FUTURES: POETRY OF THE GREEK CRISIS

Theodoros Chiotis is a poet and literary theorist. He writes poetry and code poetry in Greek and English. His work has appeared in print and online magazines and anthologies in Greece, the UK, the US, Australia, Sweden, Turkey and Croatia. He has translated contemporary British and American poets and continental philosophy into Greek and Aristophanes into English. His debut collection in Greek will be published in early 2016. He is Project Manager at the Cavafy Archive (Onassis Foundation). He lives in Athens.

T0204570

FUTURES

POETRY OF THE GREEK CRISIS

Edited & translated by

THEODOROS CHIOTIS

To Admiral James Stavridis,
Kind regards,

Penned in the Margins

LONDON

PUBLISHED BY PENNED IN THE MARGINS
22 Toynbee Studios, 28 Commercial Street, London E1 6AB, United Kingdom
www.pennedinthemargins.co.uk

First published 2015

Printed and bound in the UK by TJ International

ISBN
978-1-908058-24-9

CONTENTS

ADJUSTMENT

IMPLEMENTATION

SINGULARITY

ACCELERATION

AN OUTLET FOR A TIME OF CRISIS
WHAT TO SAY AND HOW TO SAY IT

'But there is one unfortunate difference between us [the British and the Greeks], one little difference. We Greeks have lost our capital — and the results are what you see. Pray, my dear Forster, oh pray, that you never lose your capital.'

C.P. Cavafy to E. M. Forster, 1918[1]

It might seem ironic to juxtapose the nouns 'futures' and 'crisis' in the title of an anthology seeking to map out the poetic landscape of a small country which has been in dire economic straits since the beginning of the decade. The fiscal crisis which reared its head in 2008 initially seemed like an event out of a Ballardian narrative: a man-made catastrophe unfolding in spectacular fashion and contaminating everything in its path. Of course, that is the simplistic view. We know now how widespread the crisis of 2008 was, but its impact, though felt, was not immediately apparent. Any attempt to recuperate the pre-crisis world now serves to remind us that we are only left with after-effects and persistent signs of a world that is lost.[2] As the first decade of the 21st century drew to a close, it became clear

---

[1] E. M. Forster, *Two Cheers for Democracy* (Harmondsworth: Penguin [1951] 1972), p.237, quoted in Costas Douzinas, *Philosophy and Resistance in the Crisis: Greece and the Future of Europe* (Polity Press: London, 2013), p. 19.

[2] Cf. Evan Calder Williams, *Combined and Uneven Apocalypse*, Zero Books: London, 2011, p. 35.

that the world we thought we knew was irretrievably changed. I still remember walking through the centre of Athens late at night on a Sunday in November 2009. The atmosphere was filled with tear gas and helicopters were patrolling the skies. It seemed like an inversion of the image of Zeppelins flying above Athens during the great spectacle that was the 2004 Olympic Games. It almost felt unreal.

The quoted fragment of the letter C.P. Cavafy sent to E.M. Forster in 1918 seems to have suddenly acquired a new relevance. The bankruptcy of the Greek state in 2010 was termed 'temporary' and 'orderly', which seemed like an attempt to avert the gaze from a catastrophe too hard to bear. The crisis was not simply financial; it was the dissolution of a fantasy of a world that perhaps never was. It was also a turning point for Greek public discourse. Bankspeak has since then become ubiquitous; an eroding agent in how we think of ourselves and how we think about language. It was this observation that has driven my decision to structure this anthology around financial jargon (Adjustment, Acceleration, Assessment, Singularity, Implementation). It is one small attempt to reclaim language from a semantic overdetermination imposed by the increasingly abstract processes of finance.

Manolis Anagnostakis' poem 'Thessaloniki, Days of 1969 AD' (1970) reads like an omen of a future foretold:

In any case the kids have grown, the times you knew have passed
They now no longer laugh, whisper secrets, share trust,

Those that survived, that is, as grave illnesses have appeared since then
Floods, deluges, earthquakes, armoured soldiers;
They remember their fathers' words: you'll experience better days
It's of no importance in the end if they didn't experience them, they
    repeat the lesson to their own children
Always hoping that the chain will one day break
Perhaps with their children's children or the children of their children's
    children.
For the time being, in the old street as was said, there stands the
    Transactions Bank
— I transact, you transact, he transacts —
Tourist agencies and emigration bureaus
— we emigrate, you emigrate, they emigrate —
Wherever I travel Greece wounds me, as the Poet said Greece with its
    lovely islands, lovely offices, lovely churches

Greece of the Greeks.

                                                    (trans. David Connolly)

Anagnostakis' conclusion hints at the charged, often conflicted, relationship between Greeks and Greece. The picturesque conceals a history of violence, a history in which the collective and the personal collide with often catastrophic consequences.

In his chapbook *Ouselves and the Greeks* (2000), writer and playwright Dimitris Dimitriadis poses the following, rather charged, question: 'Is it at all possible that all these things we thought about Greece were all lies, fabrications of our imagination?' The question feels more urgent than ever before. The fiscal crisis has dramatically affected modern Greek identity in the wake of a decade characterized by seemingly endless growth. Has it all been a fabrication? Is everything we thought we knew about Greece just another product of neoliberal economics?

The reality of the last few years has been sobering, to say the least. Capitalism has exploited the physical capacity of society and subjugated its nervous and psychic energies to the point of collapse.[3] Exhaustion and fatigue — concepts previously exorcised in the narrative of a booming economy — are now brought to the fore in the current narrative of crisis. The drastic changes instigated in labour management by technological and financial innovation have had a considerable impact on the social and political imagination; it is easy to infer how the increasingly volatile processes of production and value creation have initiated an erosion in the social sphere and have contributed to the widening of the gap between rich and poor.[4] It is in equal measures indicative and upsetting to think about it. The number of homeless people in Greece has risen to unprecedented levels for a European country: unofficial estimates in 2013 put the figure at 40,000 and it has risen exponentially since then.[5] The crumbling infrastructures; the harrowing stories of foreclosures; unemployment figures reaching stratospheric heights; the emergence of extremist political parties: all these events piece together a narrative of a social

---

[3] Franco Berardi, *Uprising* (Semiotext(e): Cambridge, MA, 2012), p. 66.
[4] Giuseppina Mecchia, preface to Christian Marazzi, Capital & Affects: The Politics of the Language Economy (Semiotext(e): Cambridge, MA, 2011), p.10.
[5] Alex Politaki, "Greece is facing a humanitarian crisis", *The Guardian*, February 12 2013, http://www.guardian.co.uk/commentisfree/2013/feb/11/greece-humanitarian-crisis-eu

and economic apocalypse. In this 'age of austerity', meaning has receded in the face of discursive imperspicuity.

My choice of Anagnostakis and Dimitriadis is deliberate: much like these two writers, the poets whose work makes up the anthology map out the border where the personal dissolves into the political. These poems investigate not only the blind spots and cognitive bias we all have in a time of crisis; they also incite and excavate the voices that were previously silenced.

Futures sketches out new ways of acting, talking and thinking about the present (or, at the very least, the very recent past). Written in a time of upheaval, these poems trace the transformation of personal and collective formations and the impact of these changes not only on the individual but also on the form and practice of poetry itself. There is not sufficient space to talk about every poem individually but I would like to offer some context to a few.

Stiggas' 'The Road to the Newspaper Kiosk' or Universal Jenny's 'I will now write using words of the Left' map the scope, experience and scale of the losses incurred on a personal and social level. Both of these very different poems are replete with edges, limitations, silence, non-language and gaps in their bodies. Along with Allos' 'Violent Magnesium', they investigate the limits of language and the imagination in a world where there is 'an increasing desensitization in the exchange of signs'.[6] This is very much an

---

[6] Berardi, 125.

inscription of the wound in writing.

The pictures of slogans and graffiti accompanying the five parts of the anthology underline further the underlying concern of this project: the gradual, often violent modification of contemporary personal and collective identity in a time of crisis.[7] The poems are often spoken by narrators who undergo some sort of modulation or transformation (as in Ioannidis' 'Polish', Iliopoulou's 'South', Hadzinikolaou's 'Den of Kasdaglis' or Chatziprokopiou's 'Hijras'); these texts demonstrate what it is for those who struggle to communicate on the lower frequencies without having anyone speaking for them.[8] Potamitis, Prevedourakis and Ttoouli communicate the frustration and intense affect generated by a system that seems to be running on a perpetual cycle of catastrophe.

But not all poems in *Futures* work on a macroscale. Those by Amanatidis and Apergis' 'Table' function as minute investigations of the world as occupied space, not by the desire for the transformation of the *here and now* but by a disconnection brought about by the microfascisms permeating everyday life.

Sifiltzoglou, Mayer, Critchley and Tideman borrow tropes and vocabulary from unlikely sources, their narratives becoming mirrors (in real time) of the historical and social moment we live in. In their poems, Doukas and Tsalapatis dramatize the pulverisation

---

[7] The images in the book come from my walks through Athens and are gradually uploaded on the online repository Appetite of Walls: appetiteofwalls. tumblr.com
[8] cf. Hardt & Negri, *Declaration*, 5.

of the public sphere and the signs that accompany it.

This anthology began to take shape in October 2012 in London when Tom Chivers and I were discussing the state of modern Greek poetry and how the emerging generation of contemporary Greek poets is responding to the financial crisis. In my notes from the evening, I can make out the word 'archipelago' scribbled down somewhat hastily as a gut reaction to the idea of a *generation* of poets. It is perhaps fair to say that we cannot speak of a generation in the way we thought of that term in the past. The poets in *Futures* have very different approaches to the very idea of poetry, its function and methodology. Furthermore, I decided to include in this anthology not only Greek poets but also poets of Greek descent (e.g. Critchley, Ttoouli, Willey, Sikelianos and Potamitis, amongst others) and poets who have a personal connection or affinity with Greece. The decision to widen the scope and nationality of the contributors also subverts the idea of a national or generational anthology which is destined to fail from its inception.

Instead, what this book seeks to do is to meditate on how networks, clusters and grids of poets from across the world might gather around a particular theme. The majority of these poems were written originally in Greek and translated by me (apart from the poems by Iliopoulou, Kotoula, Ioannidis and Giannisi). The undertaking of translating a variety of poets who are often quite strikingly different from one another was a challenging task for all the apparent reasons:

different poetic voices with their own inner rhythms and idioms. The translation has to transfer not only the narrative but also the pitch and tone of the original poem to the destination language: English. At the same time, it is vital to preserve the *strangeness* and *difference* of the original poem; that is to say, the attempt to bridge the linguistic divide must take into account the particularities of the narrative ecosystems and sociocultural worldviews which each poem adheres to or subverts.

Modern Greek is a language spoken by specific communities and the attempt to translate literature written in this language for a global audience runs the risk of misrepresentation in the attempt to bridge cultural and linguistic divides. The risk doubles when you are writing for the present or if you are trying to assemble a representative sample of the country's emerging poets responding to a current and traumatic event. The interesting thing about the poetry written while in the throes of the crisis, however that is defined, is that it is spurred on not so much by a conscious desire to speak about the trauma itself as it is to act as a series of meditations unique to every situation it arises from. These are poems that communicate the ever-proliferating emergencies and attempt to conceive of new strategies to connect, speak, assemble, love and survive.

Theodoros Chiotis
ATHENS 2015

THANKS

I would like to thank every poet whose work features in this book. I am humbled and honoured by your contribution, support and discussion regarding this project. I would also like to thank Tom Chivers of Penned in the Margins for his patience, support and generosity.

A personal thank you to Iliana Stamogiannou, whose support helped make the translation and editing process that much easier in the past couple of years.

A NOTE ON THE TEXT

Poems marked with † were composed in English. Poems marked with ‡ were composed in Greek and translated into English by the poet. Where a poem is marked with ¶ the translator's name is recorded at the end. The remaining poems were translated into English by Theodoros Chiotis.

FUTU RES

>

'Organise yourselves'

> ASSESSMENT

AFTER A GREEK PROVERB
A.E. STALLINGS

Ουδέν μονιμότερον του προσωρινού

We're here for the time being, I answer to the query —
Just for a couple of years, we said, a dozen years back.
Nothing is more permanent than the temporary.

We dine sitting on folding chairs — they were cheap but cheery.
We've taped the broken window pane. TV's still out of whack.
We're here for the time being, I answer to the query.

When we crossed the water, we only brought what we could carry,
But there are always boxes that you never do unpack.
Nothing is more permanent than the temporary.

Sometimes when I'm feeling weepy, you propose a theory:
Nostalgia and teargas have the same acrid smack.
We're here for the time being, I answer to the query —

We stash bones in the closet when we don't have time to bury,
Stuff receipts in envelopes, file papers in a stack.
Nothing is more permanent than the temporary.

Twelve years now and we're still eating off the ordinary:
We left our wedding china behind, afraid that it might crack.
We're here for the time being, we answer to the query,
But nothing is more permanent than the temporary.

INCOMPLETE SYNTAX
D.I.

what keeps me up at night:

the things I want to do without
unknown bits of affection
the rise of schizophrenia

I insert my future under the tongue
my future voice represents something

> perhaps a given moment
> perhaps a language-robbery

multiplies exponentially
ask for a cessation
white spaces on the page
the sound from my own throat neutral

> Mutation Of The Cry, p. 279
> p. 278, Mutation Of The Cry
> Nothing Ever Happens,
> Chapter One

devoid of meaning
I attempt to seduce
my sole evidence

REFRAIN
GEORGE PREVEDOURAKIS

Your sorrow is a poem of the street
placed on a bourgeois' lacquered shelf
a cheap elegiac couplet
a joke of decadence
at some bar at peak time
with sleeveless top and tattoos an actor-waitress
it is a dog howling inside a military camp

your sorrow is a poem of the street
crosswords on the deck, pocket-sized biosophy
on a wet cobbled road a regal beggar
a nightly gait, the border of your glance
a May wellspring to quench your joy.

NOW I WILL WRITE USING WORDS OF THE LEFT
UNIVERSAL JENNY

Now I will write using words of the Left
Because they are very nice words
I found them on a site
A word which means place

First lesson
Insurrection, four stares, transmit
Collective memory, don't talk to me about work, don't
The Afghan died, publishing houses, analytically
Giorgio Agamben, psychiatric hospital right until the end, share
this
Unfounded and therefore left behind, unwooed, Texas
Inequality, logic, dynamics
Adjustment

Second lesson
Overflowing, state of precarity, I offer my help
Too much blubbing going on
Margin, centre, in the open, or open-endedness, or even outdoors
Applied use
Over-determining left hegemony

Fortunately

I am not putting together a third lesson

You sound enigmatic, you wrote
The oppressed often seem enigmatic, I wrote back,
Like my garbage floating in the oceans of others

SHORT FILM
THEODOROS RAKOPOULOS

My homeland is a lowcost flight, it lives by sapping off shorelines like goats grazing on salt in postcards. A bailout loan drags it along, all sorts of hoists lifting its limbs, with snipers at the corners covering the procession. Doing one-takes of it, I recognize it from its bond-like form. An investment with a time horizon, surely; I accredit it androgynously, script-like. I wear vintage glasses so it can see its own reflection and treat it to mastic liqueur I had stolen for it. It lights up a fag and looks, once again through my glasses, my short film of a homeland, laden in awards at festivals abroad.

'THROUGH AN INTERNAL EXTERNALIZED / SPILL / IT BUMPS AROUND THE WORLD / TRIES NOT TO BE STUPID' (CATHERINE WAGNER)

EMILY CRITCHLEY

I'm learning about people & how to be political not emotional.
I'm learning nothing really loving — I see that — everything abstract.
I'm learning hold hold onto the people, while older people who cannot move, now the younger people move, everyone is frightened.

Something a little closed — we see that — out of the flayed
surface the TV news comes dragging emotions behind it like fear; just had
to shut up. & I'm glad. To prevent further action.
& everybody is not me not me until they want to be heard; SPACE not rights.

Nothing shared together in a human mode, only the hate hate future
— which angle couldn't be held. Because
too much pressure when everyone who wants at once.
& where I can only be sure of a wingspan to match my own (no jealous squeezing of funds / resources).

Though emotion is narrow & private
& can't be expanded. We've squandered
more air before now
in the hope
of blowing it up.

& apostasy's ripping the feathers
frm underneath
/ staking me out like stone.
While chip chip / you like this,
but chirp chirp, the day's wasting
— we're bound
to get on with it.

TRANSPARENT
THOMAS TSALAPATIS

I

It is this absurdity that tears apart the insides. All this outside invading the inside of the house and then the inside of Mr Krak. The wires brought it in, the telephones, the voices, the screens. And then Mister Krak so full on the outside becomes transparent and no one on the street recognises him. The red of the traffic light stops him. Yet on occasion someone greets him, someone transparent or some regular prankster, a crook asking for a confirmation of normality. Mister Krak grants it, perhaps unwillingly, but he is neither the first one nor the last one, he has seen it happen. He nods discreetly and that is enough. But no one has informed him, it is dangerous to go about in the city transparent. The cars try to go over you, the transparency irritates the colourblindedness of dogs, they insist on attacking, they threaten indiscriminately and the old ladies curse, like they do for everything anyway. It is difficult on the streets on transparent days. Armed with an unneeded umbrella, a silly smile and a melody repeating itself in his head for hours, Krak feels for a bit disheartened. Until the traffic light changes.

II

On this transparent night Mr Krak will hide at home.

"I will eat lightly, I will wait for half an hour to make certain that I did not have food poisoning, like after every meal, I will attempt to take a bath and then I will sleep", he thinks, in the very apartment where everything stops.

He sits on the couch and reads his book. Adrift in reflection, he feels habit telling him that he is hungry and thus makes his way to the fridge. But when he opens the freezer, a surprise awaits him.

In there, the decapitated head of a Maori, with all the geometric smudges on his face and a smile of frozen teeth, looking at him. Once he sees the head, Mr Krak thinks:

...Something odd is happening — I guess I am hungry — damn it, I forgot again to cut my hair — the head of a Maori — what are those smudges on his face? — I would like to go to New Zealand, or at the very least to Nea Philadelpheia — I guess I am hungry — where is that tasty thing whose name I don't remember? — hmm... something odd is happening, something is not going well, but what? Hmmm... oh yes, that: A MAORI HEAD IN MY FRIDGE!

And then Mr Krak's blood freezes and his face takes on a colour same as that of the Maori; a head in the freezer, a dead head, away from the dead body, that is if the body is dead as well. Who put this head in here? And how come a Maori head? They're not in season. Surprise and bewilderment burden Mr Krak. How do you react to something like this? No one has taught what sort of reactions correspond to these circumstances. And overwhelmed by novelty, Mr Krak has doubts.

A prank, a lie, perhaps a dream. In the end everything has an explanation. Maybe. Maybe someone might have left it here to come pick it up later. Maybe someone might have wanted to warn him of an impending attack or maybe someone might wanted to threaten him? He might as well lock, he might as well close the windows, he might as well turn the boiler off and hide the big table in the dining room. It won't be the first time. On the contrary, this makes the situation seem more familiar. He might as well open a book. Who knows? If he reads a little until morning, maybe the Maori will stop smiling. Perhaps he might fall asleep at some point. Yes... And curled up as he was in the dark, underneath the table, he will start to become smaller. Yes... and tomorrow morning Mister Krak will have shrunk so. Underneath the table the only thing left will be a wrinkle.

THE TRUTH
EFTYCHIA PANAYIOTOU

Life in the rubble,
your glass eyes weep centuries.
You have escaped
dreams' rags.
On the tracks of postwar bombers,
you trespass on strangers' homes.
Before the pillage you stand
defenceless.

Do not scream as the flash goes off.
/Fear seals and sews
shut the eyes of History./
The hands, do not place them on the ears.
Paleolithic lovers summon you.
Which corpse had they embraced in their wailing,
which danger squawk had pertrified their gazed
they will attest to.

Airdrops, footfalls and tears;
they hound you.
The lunacy you sought,

to upraise your head.
If you are in or out will always elude you.
But from your lungs, eavesdropper,
birds speaking foreign tongues will burst forth.

Singing you build
and solely with force,
with your chords shaking
cracking the rocks,
for a woman who —
striding on the sand
and with a spear who —
drew two snails.

You will confess, you will declare that
it was magic
(artistry
over the void)
and that she was yours,
yours when,
a riddle amongst the rocks,

once upon a time
going under.

SIMERA
ELENI PHILIPPOU

Elafonisos —
transparent the sea,
smothered in mottled starfish and black urchins.
I sit in my plastic tent, door flapping madly.
A northern wind beats back from the German nudists
who occupy the beach, penises hanging,
shrivelled crimson things.
I stare.
Each chalky pebble, round as a deficit nought.

Cheap cheap, sing the birds. The cicadas hum,
Not even your sea. Not even your sea.

*

In Attica,
from the hotel rooftop
I watch the erection of tents.

Your people carrying banners and rough signs.
They come in waves and wash the grey cement

with the paraffin grit of Molotovs.

They break upon the shoreline
of police shields,
the tainted words *drachmi* and *dollaria*.
Evro.

*

As you enter the ward you pay your *fakelaki* —
pearl-white casing for an ashen owl face —
and the doctor listens to the watery murmur in your chest,
and it beats and it beats,
but only because you paid to make it beat.

LUNA DE MIEL[1]
MARIOS CHATZIPROKOPIOU

When father "passed on" — as they say —
I returned from the tropics myself.

And we left
with mum
on a honeymoon
forty-one days later.

The rooms-to-let would not contain
the orphaned one. It was still the beginning of
May. And the only customers
were retired women from the North.
All of them, accompanied by their husbands
who were still alive.

We left
We set off

We found ourselves in the middle of a flatland.

The three girls came

---

[1] *luna de miel*: [...] Spanish [...] honeymoon [...] mensis [...] month [...]

grandmothers made of earth
— with hair in plaits —

They uttered their predictions for our lives.

The whole world came
— very kind of you, stranger!
in the space of a hitchhiking sip.

We sang sunsets

That very evening, at the mobile home
I dreamt
of a sooty fireplace
myself, the wet wood at fault
and a Saint George-Dragon
jolting me.

(disposing of me) to sparks
I was reduced.

Since then, whenever and if
I see dad in my dream
he either smiles at me
or he embraces me,

THE TABLE[1]
VASSILIS AMANATIDIS

i. [stability]

> Why so? (Why not?)
> Why not? (Why so?)
> Why so? (Why not?)
> Why not? (Why so?)

These are the four legs of the table.
This is the method of in
stability.
This is how imbalance is interpreted as stability.
This is how the table is sanctified as a construct
("and if you can't see it now, patience, you will soon see it")
and the issue is transferred to issues of territory
("we did not make the ground, it exists per se,
we are not the makers of the enveloping space").

With preconceptions such as these, we made ourselves comfortable
not on the sides, but in the corners.

---

[1] The poem is part of the larger poetic *synthesis m_otherpoem: mono logue*.

From lack of use the sides deteriorated
and we named axes some tips of lances.
When you have sat there for some time, you get used to
the tip aiming straight at you as a part of yourself.
This is convenient for everybody:
A hostility like that is not due to someone else (they all have one).
A violence like that is a universe of acquittals.

In this space, we are being kept united
by sharp tips from a face that is missing.

ii. [the merciless acquittal]

This acquittal has a coercive quality.
This is not an acquittal, it is a vaccine against guilt.
A contract with nonchalance.
We ask what is wrong, but with fraught concern we look only at the
frontage of the ground.
We ask what is wrong, but we deny any existence to our own floor
plan.[2]

United here, we are being kept together
by sharp tips from a face that is missing.

---

[2] Arrows towards the x4 centrifugal vacuum — the uniting lines incomplete—,
and not even an actual axis
where you can put your hands on and say:
here, let me stand here, in the first beginning, on my constant.

iii. [who knows?]

Such an aggregation of acquittals ends up seeming rather
suspicious.
It constantly underlines the inkling of a crime.[3]
It multiplies it, obscures it, silences it.[4]
It constitutes by itself the beginning of new crimes.[5]

So much that it becomes not guilt, but the acquittal itself
(the mother herself of all acquittals) the source
of every sin since the Creation of the World.[6]

---

[3] Whose?

[4] What?

[5] Really? But how? How and where? Whose?

[6] Really, but which? And finally whose? Please tell me, whose World?

iv. [do I need to talk about the legs as well?]

It seems for all this time we,
recognising it only by its tips,
we did not even engage in perceiving how
that which is lying inbetween us
now hovers in the air, without any legs.

Inside this space, we made a monument for togetherness,
that gradually dwindled into a furniture,
that was imperceptibly torn to pieces.
Around it now its disappearance keeps us together.

Were one of us were to step outside his corner, the table
would surely fall apart. What a shame

v. [the tree]

Our positioning around it, is what pegs it.[7]

So, how is it possible for a void to collapse?
Which absence are we protecting from falling down?

Weak and all-powerful like a mother, I rename straight away
this very acreage inbetween
the four edges of our table
no longer place, but country.

O ye, everliving hardwood,
with your traces lost in the depths of centuries,
oh you spectre-table: part of us; disabled
family tree of ours.

---

[7] Only our positioning around it, is what pegs us to the ground.

STRIP
THANASIS TRIARIDIS

Passing one night through the pedestrian area
he saw a beggar fallen in the corner
all covered with shabby clothes,
maybe he was asleep drunk,
maybe he had died.

He did not slow down his pace,
nor did he turn his face,
he glimpsed whatever he caught from the side of his eye —
the city dwellers are trained
in seeing sideways and on the move:
Inbetween the beard and the cap of the beggar
he might have seen a strip of face, maybe not.

And the next moment,
as he was walking away
(or: while the beggar was s t i l l behind him),
he thought that with this image,
with the potential strip of a face,
he could put together a poem.

ON ENZYMES AND OTHER MYSTERIES (OR WHY I NEVER PONDERED UNTIL NOW HOW LIQUEUR GOES INTO CHOCOLATE WITH FILLINGS)
IORDANIS PAPADOPOULOS

Patricia reads out loud:

Besides their soothing features well-known since ancient times, the leaves of the nepenthe plants are used today as the basic element for the production of a material (named Slips), with extraordinary nonslip features and a variety of applications in nonstick pans, self-cleaning windows, waterproof clothing, in catheters, contact lenses and lenses for sunglasses. Moreover, ecofriendly circles are investigating its efficiency as an antidote to teargas instead of Maalox, while the rivals examine the possibility of temporarily coating squares and roads with it.

and then addresses Michel (with a broken voice):

«Between sorrow and apathy I can barely stand upright»

He replies to her with verse from the Odyssey (in broken Greek):
«Then Jove's daughter Helen bethought her of another matter.
She drugged the wine with an herb

that banishes all care, sorrow, and ill humour.»[1]

Patricia palpates her thymus uneasily.
«Whoever drinks wine thus drugged
cannot shed a single tear all the rest of the day,
not even though his father and mother both of them drop down
dead,
or he sees a brother or a son hewn in pieces before his very eyes.»

She wonders if it still keeps its rosy colour.

---

[1] Translation by Samuel Butler (http://classics.mit.edu/Homer/odyssey.4.iv.html).

PERFUSION
THEODOROS CHIOTIS

1.
Yes —
perhaps in utero

    but it was in another machine

I became this:
the result of a thousand
mechanised eyes.

2.
Laura Mars
furiously click-clicking
her way into endurance.

A riot scene like magnets colliding:
the result of high population densities expanding
and then imploding across minute distances.

3.

The perfect grip of a hand
that is no longer of any use
landscapes the present.

\>

ADJUSTMENT

THE ROAD TO THE NEWSPAPER KIOSK
YIANNIS STIGGAS

Perhaps

my country still

underneath the soil

perhaps

it might still possess

a reserve of innocence

Mining is costly of course

and the perils are numerous

       many flocks of enceladi

lazy-eyed

   one-eyed

only Ioannis Kapodistrias could deal with them

he would grab them by the horns

and they would go together down into the deep

until one day he was lost

inside a large orange ore
(not like the ones they bury in landfills)

I am talking about an everlasting orange

the one that gleams on its own

and inures

the most beautiful kouroi

to ascend

to the surface again

fire lives in the death of earth,
man lives in the death of fire,

water lives in the death of air,
and earth in the death of water.

But what is the use
When somebody talks of his homeland
they throw him into the Chasm of unintelligibility

It's not like I am blaming anyone of you

It's this buggering wind

And time

Which tramples us on all fours

This is why poets always

 — this is where a line with hammers is missing —

here are some nails

as large as the instinct

not the one for procreation

but rather the one that birds have

I am talking about fluttering

inside cheap rooms

how one is enveloped

by their own flying

towards the naked lightbulb

so

that even the light
              that is artificial
is sanctified

              at some point

                        aaaahhhh

Ezra
       Ezra

When they put you in front
of the floodlights of the firing squad
and you closed your eyes tightly
the shits thought they had blinded you
How could they have known you could see
many years in the future
the x-ray of the world
with the broken knees
the shattered breastbone
and the cracks lurking slyly
inside the republics

    It's a strange thing
    It's a strange thing
    The power of evil

But the biggest irony of the crack

is neither what it does to what is to come

nor how it winters inside deterrents

It is
    that it functions like a keyhole

However much you ignore it

one day it reaches inside your eye

and then you see clearly:

Left/ only   Right/ only

That our fate   That the level
And our inexpediency   of the void
Are the same thing   does not rise by accident

But these sort of clashing rocks — Mother of God —

I got to know quite well

With every passing night

my patience loses a finger

Nine

    Eight

Seven

But once again tonight I will cross to the other side

Tonight — not for the sake of poetry

— do not think of anything heroic —

Simply
To buy cigarettes.

THALASSA
STEPHANOS PAPADOPOULOS

The road leads toward the splintered sun.
A shrub leaps into a single conifer.
Suddenly there are two conifers, then three.
They multiply into a forest.
The forest dwindles, falls in squares
of furrowed earth and farms begin.
Tobacco grows, the supple hills are brown.
They bend into the blueish mountains.
Beyond the mountains lies the water
Where the army of ten-thousand stopped,
Untied their helmets, dropped their shields,
Crashed to their knees and held their heads
At the line of curved blue water,
So wide, so deep, so dead.

WINDOWSIDE
TRYFON TOLIDES

The airport on a sunny timeless day.
Large windows. Endless squares of concrete.
Vans with little flashing lights.
Crisscrossing paths of arrival strip
and departure strip. The sun blotting out time.
The world has already ended. All of it is over,
though airplanes keep taking off
into the sky. The airport
is empty. The economy is over. I am
the only one here. Stuck, indifferent, free,
already dead. In a kind of painting.
Post-Hopper. Nameless.
No flight crews to walk through the lobbies.
Nobody en route to go anywhere.

THIS CITY
ADRIANNE KALFOPOULOU

After C.P. Cavafy (& AES)

The ruins urge you to "find another city,"
look for another shore. Even the broken finger
of a still white statue in the park points
westward. You could take that advice,
travel, find your way far from the hungry,
the shut-down stores, hope for another life.
But you're mesmerized by the ignited people
and that priest or bishop in the park
missing half his finger (who knows what his story was,
a thrown rock aimed for the statue's face
hit his raised hand instead?) — they won't leave you,
the gouged marble, the graffiti scrawls,
the statue standing like something outraged
remind you, you who yearned to live beyond this,
that hope marked you too.

PROTEST SONG, 11ᵀᴴ DECEMBER 2010
EMILY CRITCHLEY

To begin with, I am feeding a truck,
then letting the baby blow. Then slowing home
though consciously

can't hear me.
It's only things on people's lips
that's getting stuck. Not if you imitate a bird

or blue-stitched sky
wth cumuluses there.   Besides,
you bifurcate as rich, high
there,   leaping
people into   no

thing — the hard, fluffy part
that's flailingly obvious
that's at base of all calculations.
Oblaci cumulusi. Flipping greedy.

But value must be changed,
change valued. Why, there's enough,

let alone blame,   to go round
for everyone

to make distractive passions
in the dust soaring;
but sweetly, rain it
in,
all over a police's steady

fear
sudden down pour of water
/ smack / road.
Police are people too —
have so much feelings to give —

so many
days and ways: some always collide
prostrate. Others tip off
into the bluey burn
at back

of my tongue.
In the honey-for-cash
enterprise
dancing to tunes of   one

lone fuck
always wrecks

it for everyone else,
always gets in
just as soon as you've
given your heart away, ripe from

its last mending —
who have so much to give.
And I just want you to know
how we

may get along
always. And more so.
How chance,   which is great,
but can't be held fully responsible.

Humans must enter the set
at some momentary point
determined.
My last word on the matter.
Could add

pure math to the stats. But

these aery spirits make money
appear like facts
quite out of the

question.   & nothing is true
unless you
— or Descartes —
tells it so.   How is it
I just want

you to know,
tipped over like
burning. Not
act on each new now
or want now utopian whim,

felt with a zipper, unfastened.
Let's call it a revolution
of kind, really give it a name.
Each

time something becoming undone —
who have so much to give —
let's break up your staff, and go bury.

ON SUFFERING
TRYFON TOLIDES

Yearning fades, and whatever closeness you may have dreamt
or been close to having. The face fades, though some inflections
(half-remembered
or remembered for their effect—the smile brightening a place, for
example)
take longer. The scent of the person goes—
only that there was one—
a winged statue with its head and one wing missing.
The sense of the day may linger—the light and where your heart was
traveling
those days—
if such things can be made out at all.
A larger understanding comes—time-space, confusion, chaos its
terms—
the particular becomes distant, almost
a ghost. You are less distinctly connected to the other and more to all
others. Like chaos, which isn't separated from love. So being alone
exists only in a bittersweet way,
though that can bother a person dearly, while the fading goes on.
The day goes, a winged statue with head and one wing missing. The
next day comes.

IDEAL EXECUTION OF A POET
ALEXIOS MAINAS

He prefered the pen and the brush.
The sawn-off shotguns.

I still remember Giacomo Bletterstam
a frenzied fauvist I once met in Turin,
he had a twin-cylinder Vespa scooter
and an insubordinate monkey from Morocco,
we took trips to savage lakes in the mountains,
unfenced woodlands, untrammelled brush strokes,
one day in the middle of nowhere I stood in front of a junkyard to
smoke
and he painted the smoke coming out green
from the mouth of his mute monkey
like winter comes off the scooter's body.
He painted it yellow with a tulip on its lapel
as a gift to me,
it is the bullet that will get you one day, he said,
because you poets are beautiful and indisputable —
you write better inside a coffin.

One other time I chanced upon him at the protest

on the guilty factory's walls,
he did not have the painting with him
but a banner with unintelligible blobs of colour,
you are a fascist he told me in the middle of the crowd
because you believe in the world you see
(mercy exists but in the unfeasible).

A third time, at Easter, he called me to his house
where his bedridden mother
had risen to serve us overcooked goat,
we talked about the expressionists
who echo the phenomenologists,
he knew quite a bit on the issue and he was mixing it with the yellow
paint
on the oil before him,
affluence… he said, hedonism…
drawing crosses and monkeys in the air.
I had brought neither wine nor unfiltered cigarettes
and I was embarrassed to ask.

In late March I saw his unscathed scooter
in a dingy, snowed alleyway
(a German boy from Mailand astride it),

at the kiosk where I asked, someone said that he was "gone"

he was certain he met his father at the flower bed,
I asked elsewhere and one eventually comes to accept it,
a colourless fact, not something meaningful,
— what else can I say —
he died and we lost touch.

UNGODLY
ADRIANNE KALFOPOULOU

You want to flee, but flee where? The urban concrete elsewhere
does not seethe, does not breathe the scent of carob trees.
"Flee" you hear it everywhere, the taxi driver, the farmer at the
                                                        Laiki
tell you "Go!" and are puzzled that you are still here,
you who actually could — with your American passport,
your several tongues — you could translate home into longing, so
                                                why not go?
Pack your clothes, leave behind the ruined lives, elsewhere
you could lift your chin, live unburdened, "the government,
the Americans... no one cares" the taxi driver says,
and the farmer at the *Laiki* selling you the sweetest pears, advises
"Eat them cold, nearly frozen." Then shakes his head,
murmurs "*Ellada..*" this ancient land of rock cliffs,
seas that bleed their myths, Greece with its tales of flight
and light, returns, rebirths, keeps teaching the stubborn human
                                                lesson
still: the gods won't save you, neither will you stop wishing it of
                                                them,
after all you are human and they are not.

THE ADELAIDES
CONSTANTINOS HADZINIKOLAOU

In memory of Nikos Papatakis, 1918-2010

1 Animals are dying from the heat. 2 The shepherd lives in the mountains, he wants to leave. 3 He throws forcefully his crook and it's nailed to the ground. 4 His mother sells him but no one will buy him. 5 Not even Vlachopoulos, the master. 6 He has a daughter with dowry. 7 She goes and find him, he sends her away. 8 The mother has a fit. 9 The father approaches the daughter and something inside him rattles while he is looking at her neck. 10 Family life has corrupted him. 11 The shepherd learns to write. 12 He washes his feet in the river, drinks water. 13 He falls asleep. 14 He dreams of a parachute or like a pregnant goat. 15 When he awakens, the herd has scattered. 16 His dog dies. 17 He buries the dog. 18 He bids the dog goodbye, he lets it sniff his shoulder for the last time. 19 The Soldier arrives. 20 They embrace tightly, they go looking for the goats. 21 They find them, slaughtered by knife. 22 They are the ones who take them breathless to the gorge and push them over the edge as dusk falls. 23 Now they traverse plains of tobacco and the Soldier says to the shepherd, they will put you in jail now. 24 It was your doing, replies the shepherd. 25 You did all this so we might leave together once you are discharged. 26 The reservation of the poor. 27 The shepherd

shaves. **28** His mother tells him, you must kneel. **29** And only in the moonshine do their tattered clothes look almost clean. **30** He reaches the temple. **31** Everyone is gathered for the Easter Vigil and then the shepherd appears before them like a wild spectral figure and his feet put down roots in the deepest slave bow, begging for forgiveness. **32** But the crowd is moving against him. **33** The atmosphere is bearing electrical charge. **34** A hand grabs the coarse hand of the shepherd. **35** Vlachopoulos' daughter takes him away from the dark side of the village. **36** The moment she is getting ready to return to father, the shepherd becomes a shepherd of turmoil and hits the daughter in the face, tromping all over her lineage. **37** Come Despina, I will teach you not to surrender. **38** They shatter storefronts and grab meat, eggs, milk and bread. **39** The sun is coming up. **40** It smells of thyme and cold fresh air. **41** At the top of the mountain, transfigured. **42** Him: white suite, cigar, crop. **43** Her: short glittery dress, her hair has been untied. **44** Shepherd, where are you taking me? **45** My name is Thanos, I do not graze on the grass anymore. **46** He canes her calves, turns them blue. **47** Walk on Despina, the street stones harden your naked feet so beautifully. **48** On the slopes the Police and Vlachopoulos, the mother, the Soldier come together. **49** People carry lambs on skewers on their backs. **50** Oostende, Adelaide, Kiev, chortles Thanos. **51** Sweet earth awaits us. **52** The first gunshots are heard and the bullets go into the firs and are wedged in the trunks. **53** Despina surrender yourselves, father shouts. **54** Die father, Despina grabs hold of Thanos' arm wearing a bridal veil. **55** Thanos, I love you. **56** The mother gives her blessing, her son has been born. **57** They fall down the cliffs like horses without riders. **58** The afternoon sun heats up everything; **59** no one ever escaped.

THE LOVERS
EFTYCHIA PANAYIOTOU

Transformed into a wave, foaming
they let themselves dissolve.
My land, our land does not sing.
They've turned into salt.

If Hades wipes them clean with his sponge
—oh how frequently that unfortunate weeps—
wings will flare up menacingly.
Yet when we utter the king's name
we say, it cannot be otherwise, we too must have loved a little

the Underworld.

So many bodies we have caressed
we, gamins of the paternal heritage.
Our anointed limbs still glide
one within the other numb
and the lace of our pleasure, damp,
knits a face,

which is our life.

Backs turned
to the Skies, royal palaces of races (treacherous).
Treacherous geometry that will not heal.

Henceforth, entrancement.

Exiled eyelids blink
shaking off the dust.
They unfold the pages,
they unlock the prison.
A written sheet of paper is the only hell they accept
— surrounded by words,
terrified breaths on glass —,
Hell is the fiercest companion
to our centrifugal nightmares.
The dancers jump out of the speakers.
They are my fiery music.

This levitating lighthouse.
The resilient trunk of trees in the wind.
Or your skilful hands conducting silence.

LITTLE LEAD SOLDIER: BIOGRAPHICAL NOTE
PATRICIA KOLAITI

Stone or petrified tree.
When she was a child, she and her sister had
a hospital for small animals.
For years, she served as an act at a touring show:
she performed the "Big Joke".
In between military commands
she will go on hunger exercises
or tell you her story.

NICHTOPOULI (NIGHT BIRD)
ELENI PHILIPPOU

August

Night bird, night jar
Made of black down and gristle
Will you turn into a church, a tree, a house
until you morph no more?

Nesting at Skaloma by the
sea of oil, of grey stone, of old shell

We watch the clouds
The way they build
And the birds like bats
Flit and swoop. A stirring wind.

Your eyes are blue, Margrete
Do you see?

*

September

Fyssas, fyssas
on the streets of Kipselli
Do you blow out the dregs of history?
Unfeather the nest
woven of twine and bark?

I don't know, Mimi, she says on the phone
I don't know, she repeats
on the tram at Neos Kosmos.

I get off at the wrong stop.

*

October

When we first met
You took me to Exarhia
where they shot him.
Dried out carnations and graffiti
A tree with rose pomegranates

We met your father in the street

outside his shop. A hole in the wall,
Concealed while they riot and break up Athens.
He remembered Asimos rolling a wheel
Down the street back in the 70s. *The madman*, he laughed.

*

November

As a little boy you would roll oranges
Into the road, under car wheels.
You started your own political party with Pavlos and Magdalini.
The three of you, tiny and so serious,
put up hand drawn posters
on the streets of Brahami.
The neighbours still remember it.

*

December

I needed to suffer to see you.

It didn't sit, the words didn't catch, the soul didn't hear
And the heart, it hardened and broke. I was dead to your story, to the

acts and the snow and the cold of the old winter clock.

You told me that you didn't love me like you used to, and that you thought I didn't love you at all.

The country changed, we changed.

LAZIENKI
PANAYOTIS IOANNIDIS

The squirrel kept sniffing in the wet grass
Its bushy tail irritated the peacocks
that strutted around screeching
Among the flower-beds, on the verandas
their claws stabbed at the stone slabs

The last king, Poniatowski, slept uneasily
Ryx, his trusted companion, lay awake next door
A humble barber from Flanders
personal guard, manager, at last a nobleman
his coat of arms, a Ring

The little Water Palace unsuspecting
bridged the lake
A few years hence the country would be torn in three
Half a century a later, swiftly and soundlessly
arisen from their barracks at the Park's other end
the select young men of Archduke Konstantin, the Russian
would cross the pavements
He, disguised as a woman, fled
But one more uprising drowned in blood

In thirty years' time
the Kingdom of Poland
was erased

In black, the women sold
hid their jewels
They put on
iron chains

HEADS OF SATYRS[1]
DIMITRA KOTOULA

'I did only Satyrs. I wanted to stop that sarcastic laughter
that made me go mad.'

        Yannoulis Halepas, 1878

I have every right to be alone
— a minute presence —
I alone have every right
to observe
the well-crafted volumes
the black grimaces on this marble.
I want to understand
(try to understand)
what it is that hastens to give the brain its freedom
what — in extreme refinement —
it is that asks the brain to give back its freedom
the whole story
the scenario and the hammer.

---

[1] In the winter of 1877-1878 the famous Greek sculptor Yannoulis Chalepas suffered
from a severe nervous breakdown: he destroyed hundreds of clay models, studies and
sculptures, mainly of heads of Satyrs. He was put 'under observation' and, ultimately,
sent to Italy to recover. He soon returned to Greece to study the sculpture of the
Acropolis but ended up in a public psychiatric clinic on the island of Corfu.

The artist tried to do this.
It is 1878.
The Acropolis exists.
This country exists (exists?)
"*under observation*" — be it so —
and "*in deteriorating condition*"
the face filtered through the wrinkles
(he might almost guess the agitated movements passing by
the holograms on this marble)

Whatever exists will be destroyed

every single clay model
every single study
the soul exposed
to this impulsiveness
overwhelming the empty air (empty?)
the air filled with empty agitation
don't turn around/   don't believe it/
don't deceive your mind with ghosts of this kind

I have every right to be alone
I alone have every right
to observe
this face

the laugh on this face
eroding consciousness
projecting elastic
the whole face a laugh
drenching/   years now/   the mind/   bending it
to the point of utter resistance
where only the wind can bend.

The world becomes smaller and smaller — almost empty.
(what is the true primal essence of things)
The mind stops resisting.
The hands remain inert.

I have every right to be alone.
I want to stop this laughter.
I want to hear beyond it.

Translated by Richard Pierce

THOSE DAYS
ADRIANNE KALFOPOULOU

Those days we woke up almost excited
though not with joy, wakeful like an animal
alert to a danger it can't see, but can sense

in the tension of the air those days we walked
straighter than usual, aware of the
smallest movements around us, the drug addicts

leaning into each other as if their spines
had collapsed, scratching a scab,
the way we felt, but unlike them we kept walking,

ignoring our hurt, the garbage stench like a
rotting cat, trash piled up from the strikes
those days the refugees from Africa

couldn't always spread their wares,
as the pavements gathered the party youth
who hung their banners from statues and trees.

Even the statues those days wore stoic looks

as they bore their spray-painted mustaches, their added nipples,
weary citizens like the rest of us

shouldering a weight as outdated revolutionary
songs blared from megaphones set up by
the party youth who still cared for Communism and its hopes

as they sang lyrics from the poems
of Ritsos, from the songs Theodorakis once sang
to inspired followers and patriots, but today

we think of those days as long gone
as we hand over spare change to respectfully dressed men
who apologize for their begging and explain

they are desperate, with families. Today, we think
it will take a small miracle to save us
since we know it is no longer enough to do our duty,

pay our bills. "Those days" we will say, if we are lucky,
to grandchildren and young friends, "people died in Greece,
not because of war but because some did not see

the enemy, or recognize it in time."

DYNAMITES
THEODOROS RAKOPOULOS

Every time I die, the stalagmite grows unseen at the far end of the cave grows, where I descend with fresh new drops, to show the crystals where you beam like an insect's dark vision. You beam a thousand faces, Little Porcupine, like an insect's dark vision. My deaths, the way things are going lately, come every two or three months, regular like dentists, and with credentials for their come-back, thanking for the hospitality. But the geological speeds in the caves drip thousands of tears, salts dissolving by the centuries.

How poor you are, o deaths of mine. At school trips, hands are hiding you in pockets like mementos — you linger behind, dying from the beginning all the time.

How poor you are, how insufficient. Do you not hear, the TNT that goes off in the depths of the stagnant waters at the edge of the cave, and outside the siren of the school bus, accompanied by songs, tapes, and go to hell you brats, the speleological associations will put us all in jail.

\>

IMPLEMENTATION

THE NAIL
THOMAS TSALAPATIS

This thing started growing on the forehead, this thing, just like they had warned me. In the beginning it was like a spot or perhaps a mole that you can forget even for a short while. But then I started headbutting people, and that hurt quite a few of them. A nail was all it was, a nail started growing on my forehead. Perhaps to others it might have happened before, but for me it was the first time and every time it grew a centimetre it was once again the first time for me. As it was growing, it made my head squeak like time-worn wood flooring. And yet I feel no pain, no more than when my nails or hair are growing. I have heard that nails and hair keep growing even after death, I would like to know what is going to happen with the nail, I cannot guess. Fortunately, the attitude of the people around me did not change — except that no one wants to headbutt me anymore. What I mean to say is that no one really liked me. And now instead of them saying "there goes that tosser", they say "there goes that tosser with the nail on his forehead". I would not call that a change.

Sometimes, while I am sitting quietly in the park, a bird comes to rest for a bit on the nail. I drive it away with a mechanical movement. I look at people, the old men with the kites, the homeless, the women with the buggies and the children inside the buggies. I ponder, some people prefer boys, others prefer girls, while I prefer the buggies. It's nice to have a choice.

Then the doctors came. They started to talk to me in a calm tone. They reassured me. They had no reason to do this. I was not the one who called for them. They took me from the park. They took me to a big building and the corridors smelt of detergent. They started convening amongst themselves. I was waiting outside the room, motionless for two or three days. Arguments, deliberations, comparisons with other phenomena, diagrams, charts, questions, answers and queries. I saw someone faint, one other person respond positively. I saw someone behaving anxiously, someone walking indifferently. Answers, answers, answers.

One day they lay their friendliness on my shoulders with reassuring hands — they had no reason to act otherwise. They said various things to me. I don't remember them. They finally announced their decision to me.

After a thorough and elaborate inquiry they decided that a nail is growing on my forehead. For this reason they decided to take measures. They hung a painting on my forehead. A painting that now covers my face. I do not remember how I felt, but from their reactions people seemed relieved, enthused, I might even call some of them content.

It's been a while since then. The nail has stopped growing. And the painting is still hanging there. Everything is quiet behind my frugal adornment. The only bad thing is that I cannot see — to be fair, it's not like that there is anything special to see. These days I pass my time in the park, quietly on a bench, with my face behind the painting listening to voices, footfall, buggies. But be warned: I am in a state of readiness. I am standing by for someone curious enough to move the painting to see what is hiding behind it. Then I, prepared for sometime now, will scream at him briskly, robustly, vigorously. I hope I am able to frighten him. I am certain, yes…his reaction, will make me laugh. Honestly I have not laughed in a while. I am just spending my time behind the painting and in vain I am trying to imagine what it represents and what it depicts. With eyes blocked up, I am daydreaming of its vistas, with eyes blocked up I am putting together its acreage.

AUSTERITY MEASURES
A.E. STALLINGS

If you believe the headlines, then we're sunk.
The dateline oracle, giddy with dread?:
"Greece downgraded deeper into junk."

Stash cash beneath the mattress, pack the trunk.
Will drachmas creep where Euros fear to tread?
If you believe the headlines, then we're sunk.

A crisis that lasts for years? — call it a funk.
Austerity starves the more its maw is fed
And downgrades all our deepest bonds to junk.

Every politician is a punk:
The right, the left; the blue, the green, the red;
Ministers in cahoots with the odd monk.

We've lost our marbles — Elgin took a chunk —
Caryatids, gone on strike, sit down instead;
Teargas lingers like a whiff of skunk.
.
Weep, Pericles, or maybe just get drunk.
We'll hawk the Parthenon to buy our bread.
If you believe the headlines, then we're sunk:
Greece downgraded deeper into junk.

BLOOD POEM
STEVE WILLEY

That half of my blood is called Greek is this poem
That under microscopical

Obligation is seen to reek its contrite and unsatisfactory
Lubrication on some conjured career that sieges

Back as dirty echoes of misplaced hope approach historic thickets
of forcible
Migrations.

That half of this poem is called Greek is my blood
That stops to issue crude guesses

As to the shape of her inner thighs under the violet disco
Light, my grandmother, glistening in rhythmic anticipation

Of my mother, her soon to be cinnamon eyed arrival, under the
strip-lit skies
Of Mombassa.

That half my poem is called blood is this Greece
That tugs at the lungs to the back of the heart and out

Through the bone of the spine and the cheek, that turns late as a
swan
In the thread-red seeps that wet the white, which cruel as money,

Offers its ignorant song of hurt to what is left of Greece is left
Of me.

That half of my Greece is called blood is this poem
That stretches radical, uncountable and serried in rows of book
blocs all aflame

In the victorious matriarchal night, sharing their cinders in deep
ravines of love
That feel in the body like my mother, who in her French accented
thought

Considered the question of the crimson arrival of plums in the clot-
tooth
Mouth of her new and most desolate queen.

That half of my blood is called Greek
     Is this poem.

That half of this poem is called Greek
     Is my blood.

DEFLECTION
KIRIAKOS SIFILTZOGLOU

the decision makers would deflect if they could
they would deflect even bolts of lightning
from the centre to the periphery   where
bullets fall when the dark
falls and the roosters crowed

                          a long time ago

EPID/ONEIROS
SOPHIE MAYER

this is the chamber full of snakes
    walls will not fall
prescription, Aesculapian: catharsis

to awaken
         cleansed
                of
nightmares (& by them).

the venom :: pharmakon
    start
    stop
       the heart
(carry on in this vein &)

underground, palpitating, we are yards
from that kitten-in-the-litter-bin
called theatre
what can the matter be / stone
uploaded to the digital amphi

that gap where the world gets in
we are what enters
the unseeing circle & prises its eye
openopenopen

to the sky / we are bodies
on the line of mountains, mouths
agape
        / agapē amid this pothos : strife
that rises from s/kin
if I :: then you :: are they
        there are no walls to fall here
        but in our (tholos) thumos

we (un)build what buries
                        is buried in
us

Beat.

S/he
exits into the skēne; the long sharp
of it (bronze pin, Archeological
Museum Catalogue #: redacted [WMD]) already in
our breasts

eyes

"At the performance of *Persae*, it is reported, women fainted and miscarried. Athenian playwrights were thereafter banned from using recent events in their plays."

Konstantinos Georgousis, codename Aeschylus,
irises his lens, saying: drink this
(bitter) (emetic). Look,
the tarnishdark of dawn has passed.
Now: the work of morning.

SURVEY: PHOTOTROPES
ELENI SIKÉLIANÒS

The snow falls, picks itself up, dusts itself off
a sparrow flying like a leaf back up to its tree
The future does a backbend toward you, it's
what you can almost see, scrimmed
in the clouds which crowd the sky, elbowing, laughing

After that I see space and its influence in a bucket of spinning water
and two calcium atoms shoot forth, twinned photons traveling

back to back, arms unlaced, perfect
swimmers in the lit dusk

Where are they going?

First, to Holland, then
to calcium-kiss her bones

And in Holland the streets are made of water, the dolls & dogs
gather
  round lit picnic tables like happy rags

The body is in the root cellar

When snow falls our dead gather close to our bones
because the cold's ghost has come back to haunt the cold & the
body,
too, is a happy rag

Tree, take a photograph of her thought, you can do it
with photosynthesis: silhouettes of seals appear, a swarmed planet
and its satellites, a
    celestial atlas that breaks when tapped (it's glass)
Some giraffes, some elephants, a lion scatter
in the clearing; in the clearing

the leaves of the world turn toward the light as do the letters of the
word
the words are beautiful not for their accuracy but for their dream:
words-are-arrows that loop between no-man's-land and the
wetlands, soft
flints flying toward their target

— words bird the zone —

when home was adopted as mother
area was given here
[a future of] all surface, no border

AMMUNITION POEMS
THEODOROS RAKOPOULOS

*

Whichever stone I might turn over
I find you underneath.
Any way you look at it, you must have been
stoned.

*

They shot you in the shoulder. But the bullet was an exploding one
and articulated in a quasi-archaic lingo, like the novels of Jules Verne
— "without a match." Thus the entire page collapsed with it. Upon
the tearing of the page, the reader turned around and ducked.

*

The voice of the poet, bodiless:
Plugged into the metallic recording
Without an organic soundsystem
Straight from Kalvos' wireless throat.

*

Marfin blues

We look at our own hand
Crossing through to the other dimension
Just seconds ahead, wound up
It passes us the baton
(We barely touch it): carbonised —
This revolution hails from some other land. Delete the date.

THE BUTANE HEART OF TRISTAN TZARA
STERGIOS MITAS

1

The divine bark covers the verses. Nevertheless: it is rain that makes the clock of organised poetry tick. The beauty of your face is a precision timekeeper. You are beautiful, Clytemnestra, the crystal of your skin awakens our gendered curiosity. You are soft and calm, like two meters of white silk. Clytemnestra, my teeth are clicking. You are married. I am cold, I am scared. I become green, I bloom, I keep time on the butane gas, I am scared. When will you have the pleasure to see the inside jaw of my revolver? To close upon my lung of chalk. Without any hope for a family.

2

Exceptionally sensitive to the punishment of your droplet, I decided to turn off the faucet. The hot and cold water of my charm will not be able to soothe the sweet results of your sweat, the love of the heart or the love lasting only a few minutes. The lay people protest for a home, the important people protest for a monument. "Where", "how", "why", these are monuments. Like for example: Justice. What a fair and orderly function, almost like a nervous tic or a religion.

3

Clytemnestra, the wind is blowing. On the quays with the ornate bells. Turn your back and stand against the air. Your eyes are gravel, they cannot see but the rain and the cold. Clytemnestra. Have you felt the horrors of war? Can you slip into my sweet language? Do you not breathe the same air as me? Do you not speak the same language? On which invaluable metal have the fingers of your discontent snagged? Which mysterious curtain filters music, which music prevents my words to wedge in the wax of your head? Certainly, the rock gnaws at you and the bones hit your bones, but language, randomly segmented in slices, with its white manners will never be capable of unleashing within you a stream. One night, digging into night, we found in the depths a smallish night. It was called goodnight.

4

Absentminded the thief was transformed into a suitcase — the physicist, thus, can argue that the suitcase stole the thief. The waltz continued as always (forever continued no longer), the waltz was playing — and the lovers ripped off pieces as they were passing through; an old wall does not deserve posters anymore. Clytemnestra, you are beautiful. I love you with the lucidity of a diver (his algae). My blood is quivering. Your eyes are blue. Why don't you hear, Clytemnestra, the quiet laugh of my cells, the violence of my breath and the sweet childish possibilities that fate has in store for us? Were you perhaps expecting from my constitution other sensual revelations?

5

Its tick-tock was giving us the sniffles. A little death for the tick-tock of its life. We have time, alas, we are not short of time. Time has a moustache (like everybody else), even women and the shaven Americans. Time is tight — the eye is evil — but in any case it is not the wrinkly pouch of the miser. The wind gives a jolt, a curtain of the void: its stomach is filled with so many foreign coins. The void drinks the void: the wind came and it has blue eyes, this is why it is constantly swallowing aspirin tablets. Once a day we abort our darknesses.

THE KING'S NEW CLOTHES: A VARIATION
MARIA TOPALI

I

Always according
To the fairy tale known to all,
The king was naked.

Only things happened a little differently.

He did appear stark naked
During an official festivity
But not because he was purportedly tricked
By some scalper.
His nudity, well known to himself and to his environ,
Was power's silverware.
With it he humiliated everybody:
Both to see him in a way they did not wish to
But also to refute the very thing.

Until one day that child
Came close to blowing everything sky high!
This is how it always happens.

It is enough for someone to dare first
— even if it's a child.
Then everyone else follows.

II

The archcardinal
Was a man of wisdom.
Of course he
Might have been emptying every morning
the master's potty
but he was, in all other respects,
richly educated and all-powerful.

He let the first storm pass.
There was rioting, barricades were put in place.
The cardinal negotiated,
Gave out money, promises.
Things settled down.
As time went on the image of the heroic child
Started to grow pale.

Who was he, in the first place?
A child who would intimate
That up until then we were all without exception subjugated?

Word started getting round
That the child was arrogant.
Spiteful and superficial and careless
— "of course the king was naked" —
Was repeated without end.

Until someone (he later won distinctions and honours in his field)

said, in a taverna, one evening:
"Well, I recall him wearing socks".
Then another one added: "Me too! I seem to remember something,
weren't they blue?"

Thus, it was reconstituted gradually
Out of nothing
the entire outfit of the king
and they lived happily.

III

You're probably wondering: what about the child?
The child was segregated
And his talents were disputed.
He fell, as they say, "into disfavor".

Depression, memory loss, same old.

One day
He gathered all his courage
to pick up
boldly
with both hands the bags from the supermarket
and to go through the till barrier.

With Sphinx-like eyes, the Medes waited for him
On both sides:

«Hello, Leonidas!», they greeted him. «How are you feeling today?»

December 2012

THRIFTSHOP
GEORGE PREVEDOURAKIS

Leafing through the upper edge
of silence
inbetween all those vaccilating mouths
tell us

    if you are in danger.

POLISH

PANAYOTIS IOANNIDIS

Unfathomable
this love of Jan Sobieski
for his enemy's beauty

Every day for twenty years
he'd write to his wife
half in Polish and half in French
And about the Turkish spoils outside Vienna
"des fort jolies choses et fort riches
mais fort riches"

Among all of Hussein Pasha's treasures
he fell in love with a silk embroidery
"with two thousand rubies and emeralds"
He loved it so
he draped it over his horse
on his coronation day

Indebted to the Grand Duke of Tuscany
he parted with it
The Duke had it taken down
in the register and stored —
"Una cosa del barbaro lusso"

PLAKOTO[1]
GEORGE PREVEDOURAKIS

Every September the verbs fester
who reordered your letters my homeland?

---

[1] Plakoto is a table game popular in Greece. The object of Plakoto is for the player to bring all their checkers around to their own home board and then bear them off. The player who bears off all of his checkers first wins the game.

'National Republic of World'

\>

SINGULARITY

INTERNATIONAL MAIL
KIRIAKOS SIFILTZOGLOU

Jasper, had you ever seen the flag of the volunteer unit of the Greek-Americans during the 1912-1913 wars? Had you seen rags transforming in time into works of art? Did you imagine decay as a slow stroke of the brush, gunpowder as a livid transitory shadow, the distance of the visual as the range of a gun in a battlefield, the torn threads as a reflection of the intensity of shattered nerves, the lost pieces of fabric as the theory of the lost centre, whichever holes you came across as black wells of the subconscious?

Jasper halt! Who art thou? Were you a precursor without your knowing it or will time and nature always surpass you? Time grabs you by the hair, Jasper, and you do not have the time to comprehend the exact moment you become an oil painting. Your bones, Jasper, they could have been the pole of a flag. I wonder about your experience of the American civil war. Were you with the South or with the North? Were any of your ancestors killed? Does the phrase "friendly fire" ripple through your work? What do you prefer, the raising or the lowering of the flag? Does "half-mast" remind you of something?

Jasper, I might have worn you out, so stand at ease. You know, they say that this is the Balkans, and this is why we tend to burn flags, we do not come near rags, here place is time and time is place but we are out of time and place. Yourself, where are you? Are you mainly your image or are you your source material as well? Do you play, and if you do, do you take it to the extremes? Your signifieds, do they reach the bottom or are they floating on stagnant waters? Is there a back door to your avantgarde? For real, Jasper, do you see flags in your sleep or are you mocking us? In any case, to finish with this, perhaps our skin might be our only flag.

THE BOX
THOMAS TSALAPATIS

I have a small box in which someone is always being slaughtered.
It is a little larger than a shoebox. A little less elegant than a box with
cigars. I do not know who, I do not know whom, but someone is
being slaughtered in there. And you cannot hear a sound (except for
the times when you can). I place it on the library, on the table when
I want to spend my hours looking at it, away from the windows so
the sun won't discolour it, underneath my bed when I want to feel
naughty. Inside it someone is being slaughtered, even when we have
a celebration in our house, even on Sunday, even when it's raining.

When I found the box — I am not going to say how, I am not going
to say where —, I brought it home satisfied. At that time, I thought I
heard the sound of the sea. However, in there massacres are taking
place.

I started to be sickened by the noise, the knowledge of the events,
the events inside the box. Its presence started making me sick. I had
to act, to liberate myself, to calm down, to take a bath. Decisions had
to be made.

So, I mailed it to a friend; a friend whom I keep only to give gifts to. I wrapped the box in an innocent-looking colourful cardboard with an innocent-looking colourful ribbon. Inside the mailbox there is a box and inside that box someone is being massacred. Placed inside the mailbox, it is waiting to arrive in the hands of a friend. A friendship I maintain solely for gift-giving.

MUTILATED IMAGES
GEORGE TTOOULI

In Lefkosia I watched a cockroach
walk beneath the barricade.
My battle scars unhealed
and the wounds started
oozing.
          A red dawn
on the milky sands —
Why so sour? What do
you warn me of?
What are you trying to say?

I write to try and close them:
There was a man from Cyprus
whose wounds were oozing pus.
He lost his faith
in nationhood.
Is there something we need to discuss?

In Lefkosia I watched a cockroach
crawl beneath the barricade.

Some images arrest you,
take you out of the house
hours before dawn
into the street with a rifle to your head
so you can mark the make
on the barred: MADE IN US

some images set fire to your homes
and wait by the well s for the men

Some image line the village
women in the street
lift their skits up with bayonets
and stab them in their stomachs
when the women slap their faces

While other images take you into the dark
between two huts and rape you
and rape you again

and some images raise many questions
while some questions don't have any answers
and other images cannot be answered back to

and some images return to me mutilated

and some images return to me mutilated
and some images return to me mutilated

In Lefkosia I saw a cockroach
reaching for a Molotov.

No, that's not right.

In Lefkosia I socked a rock
and swung it at a soldier.

In Lefkosia the crawl of progress
crashes into barricades.

In Lefkosia I cocked a gun
and breached the bloody barricade.

In Lefkosia the hotrod preachers
speak of flaming hurricanes.

In Lefkosia the twilight sky
wakes up to stark incendiaries.

In Lefkosia electric pylons
fade into statistics.

In Lefkosia a dirty language
crawls along the tenements.

In Lefkosia the UN line
encroaches on our merriments.

In Lefkosia there's nothing holding
insects to the barriers.

In Lefkosia they open fire
on politician's motorcades.

In Lefkosia I threw my passport
on the burning placards

What? What am I trying to say?

In Lefkosia I watched a cockroach
crawl beneath the barricades.

HIJRAS[1]
MARIOS CHATZIPROKOPIOU

Black rags of grandmothers
saint napthalene of hallowed closets
the wood on the floor creaking
the little balcony on the verge of collapse, a spectre
the new owner
will coat with cement.

Black rags of grandmothers
wooly heat at midday
your scent like a quilt
and a cool breeze
you dampen my unfathomed night, the night that is of age
you scratch at my snakebodice.

—Please do not forget to name me I Return

I Give birth, a bare sweet homecoming!
in(to) your vagina I creep

---

[1] *hijras*: Hindi (হিজড়া,) and Urdu (ہِجڑا) [...] Southasian cultures [...] male biological
gender [...] female social identity [...] 20th century [...] activist hijras [...] Western
NGOs [...] official recognition [...] third sex [...] categories [...] beyond [...] Etym.
arabic root *h–j–r* : abandon, denounce, migrate

I take on your form
and we start to
dance

Three widowed Graces

My male head, a freshly prepared treat
on the platter
we tear each other's hair over who will tongue kiss it

Joy to your seven veils!

GRAPHĒ DECEMBER
NICK POTAMITIS

Any kind of bloodletting pre-Christmas
smacks of gash telenovela
trope-farming run amok ; sophistry slashfic
like Simone Weil as Carmen
In Guangzhou pulverising your noblesse
oblige . The blood spilt warms itself
& everything is in too sharp relief .
O wonderworking bronze save our
sons at least from the bloody savage &
all other first-person shooters .

•

Gas & flame & motors turning-over
burnt out engines of agonist
habitus disturbing all that remains ;
all that fiasco loot overreaching
beyond doctrinaire resentment
to the blazing craic & razzle .
From high on squat panopticon
Kid Ajax bristling bides his time

as empire summons its' blame battalions
outsourcing shameface & punish .

•

A fifteen year old who once was not dead
is now . Everything points downwards .
The torpedo'd social contract ; of lowriding
your slacks like a cholo
gangbanger reading Marx till the zone
becomes breachable invoking
ethic consequence unbroach'd by either
side . Marketable eros plus
massacre in the polytechniki
is its' own brutalist divide .

•

Down from their stratify'd elevations
schoolkids obliterate patrolcars
dispensing swerving bloc-votes of noconfidence
in futureal
payback & scrolling frantic to void vast
dinosaur-splitting asteroids .
Null dispensations pay out only harm

& boom-timers renege sans guilt
till levelling up is not an option ;
just keep the blast'd spheare in play .

•

That rank anti-rocker necromaton
foaming to scorch the fire-starters
gets as blast'd apart as the bodyshock'd
indignados he abjects .
Ignore the flame war & instead ignite
symmetrically align'd wreckage
firing up provocative analogues
from the potato farm to the art hub .
A dream'd of gift economy that sparks
over us like Attic wildfire .

•

Skill'd resource management of game tokens
& Israeli tear-gas is key
to ending the month stockpiling the win .
December leads the way over
crack'd glass & blanket shrapnel of normal
class roles ; a proud subtle limbo .

Then Kid Ajax weighs in with colossal
stoney uppercut collapsing
the chic computer megastore atop
everybody ; hi-score intact .

•

Refute the usual attribution
of cargo-cult banality ;
the usual over-invest'd smacktalk
binaries of Red versus
Blue . The archive insists that young rebels
depatriate to Tashkent &
the junior shoppers to our Queen's most kind
Kinderlager . Players risking
amity as a new mode of being
exceed the limits ; a commons .

•

Something happens but must keep happening .
Moments yearn to persist ; a wish'd
for irruption of the unbuilt against
dense ambient normality
that weighs . Concussion grenades can do one ;

a Mummers' Play amongst dice &
Emo's grubbing at throwing-stones & skate
royalty hurling themselves square
against gravity & the phalanx for
defunct Fredy Villanueva .

•

Megalexandros is this Decembrist
excess ; this fleeting transcendence
of commonweal prose terrain that prescribes
barely living as status quo .
The huge Christmas tree is on fire despite
the de-sanctify'd common room .
He lives so let them demonise nomad
freebooters aestheticising
life crisis ; pseudo nodal points calling
for one last nativity truce .

IN THE STYLE OF Y.S.
YIANNIS STIGGAS

I am permanently dreaming
of an uphill slope leading straight
   into your insides
of going in and changing the algorithms
so that the heart
bedazzles thinking thoroughly
Αγχιβατείν[1] — *Pallaksch*[2]
as my grandfathers used to say
(stamping their feet on must)
darkly intimating

 Blood is in our future
and how can one dance to it

*

---

[1] *Αγχιβατείν*: Refers to fragment 122 of Heraclitus referring to the dialectic relationship
between existence and non-existence (Ed.).

[2] *Pallaksch*: Refers to the poem 'Tubingen, January' Paul Celan wrote about philosopher
Friedrich Hölderlin. 'Pallaksch' was uttered by Hölderlin in his dementia, in his last
years of his life spent in the home of a Tübingen carpenter; it could signify Yes or No
(Ed.).

Perhaps
if a man came along today
bearing the asset typical to the times
this particular flavour of a makeshift precipice
— you understand —
one of the thousands apprentices
of panic
while God was stitching them together
he forgot a needle inside their chests

If he came
and looked

through the eye of the needle I was telling you about

all of his vowels would become haunted
and a stuttering would stump his mind

n-n-n-n-n... n-n-n-now t-t-t-t-t... t-t-t-that
t-t-t-t-t-t-t.... t-t-t-t-th-th-things.... h-h-h-h-have.... b-b-b-b-become
 t-t-t-t-t-tou-tou-tough.... d-d-do-do... y-y-y-you... th-th-th-th-think
t-t-t-...
t-t-that the-the-the... the-the-the-the... the l-l-l-l-l.... l-l-l-l-li-li-light
u-u-u-u-u-u... u-u-u-un... u-u-u-und-und-u-u...
u-u-u-un-un-understands?

*

Of course I have no answer at all

so I shrug my shoulders like all of you
with that old
shortcoming of mine of spring
I am still not done with
and I let my neck be grazed on
— those red marks
are not —alas— from kisses

they call her suffocation that so-and-so

but
    it is not poetry that places the noose
but
    it is poetry to that kicks at the stool

*

Because poetry
— *hey, big guy* —
is not a trapeze of daydreams

it is not your flying pet
— *hey, big guy* —
When you impersonate the moon
you should also impersonate it when it's waning
— I will not make it any clearer for you —
If you can understand this
that's good
otherwise
Boy, you are in dire need of Mayakovsky

*

Where might you be now, Vladimir,
now that both of our Nobels
   have become clashing rocks
No one is setting sails any longer for the journey
no one is sailing for the blue
it frequents all on its own in great altitudes

and old loves

*

Dora
  Konstantina

Evanthia
Everytime I change sides in my sleep
they silently unwind my star sign
until never becomes
our lucky number
— what a Russian roulette, Mother of God —
you know of these things, Vladimir,
it happened
it happened in Odessa

wait till you see what is happening here

*

Here
the evil eye is working overtime
I apologise for writing this but
we turned light into
the perfect hideout — *for nothing* —

—what else do you want me to say—

last night at the metro
thousands of bodies were touching
and not even a spark was lit to save face

not even a tiny electron
something
to make the blank stares shudder

in the hope that we might see Ithaca stark naked
underneath the dinner suits
                         and the shirts

It can drive you crazy

the way the days and nights are unravelling
your blood one thread at a time
your three fates turning white
what are you expecting to *begin,* you nincompoop,
this is not a fairytale

it is

only its carcass

                              *

The tragedy of my homeland
If you of course exclude the earthquakes
all the other —isms

have sold us off shamelessly
My good lord Byron,
you suffered the exit for nothing
you lit the way to the exit for nothing
your fever these days
barely exists in the manuscripts
they have donned him with some squalid microbes
while he was purely valiant
a Christ registering an eight on the Beaufort scale
and probably even more than that

Then — lost amidst the reeds
now — lost amidst the cheap nightclubs

*

THIS IS THE PLACE GENTLEMEN

Many fathoms underneath nothing
so
that our hair is tangled in its roots

O Absalom, my son my son

as a pendulum you would not have a lot going for you

either way we
import our time from Greenwich

because our time
has gaps black and unfilled
you shout love
and the echo comes back covered in blood

there are millions of hands which were cut off
they did not belong to statues
        all of them
later turned to stone

*

What irony is this, Vladimir
If you were to come today
I might not have been able to hear you
I live on a busy street
sirens honks
My hearing a total mess
— no, I am lying to you —
it is loneliness
that puts me since I was little at full blast
this is why my most faithful lines

the miracle is a precipitous swallow
   or
come on Konstantina, tell me
how is it possible
that you are not here
            and yet it's a full moon

(and a lot of other things
darker than the unfulfilled)

give me audio feedback in my sleep
and I sleepwalk
with the acerbity that dreams have
in my silly pyjamas

o if I could properly collapse
in a proper sunrise

in the hopes that I too might genuinely shout

Αγχιβατείν – *Pallaksch*

The starburnt spectre
which perfectly depicts me.

EPITAPH
YIANNIS DOUKAS

'... because the statues are no longer debris,
we are.'
George Seferis

We turned off the lights after all of this,
you gently leaned on me and said:
"We shall live stitching with a thread
the holes of history; whatever was before this

can never be restored".
At least, that "before",
as events negate it forevermore,
we should reject that too. What is to be stored

on this earth, in the present
out of all this rumination
whose remaining breath leads us to our obliteration
at the same time we turn our backs to what is everpresent?

We lay wreathes and weep,
but we are what we burn, we are what we bury deep.

WHY BECAUSE
ELENI SIKÉLIANÒS

WHY BECAUSE the lost cat ate tiropita from my hand
why because I can see the other side of Lesvos from here
why because I saw Sappho in the rocks by the harbor saying plash
plash Aphrodite
how could anyone not gorge always goddess and gorgeous
Sappho was looking great, profiled out to the east
why because of course the miraculous bees
They are surviving here they are
Surviving here

THE BOOK IS THE HOUSE
ELENI SIKÉLIANÒS

THE BOOK IS THE HOUSE where the bodies are buried
the book is the catacombs where the corpses enumerate
the book is the joy is the place were the copses unfold happy, fragrant,
& shining
the book is the meat sliding inside the bear and the bear inside its
blanketing fur
the book is the joy was lost on the horizon
as hours flooded in
the trees kissed across the distances, & the sun
mirrored
in its pages the lake
therefore lung-ed as any animal I leaf
the wide pages flammable with life

WE MAKE A POLIS
EMILY CRITCHLEY

WE MAKE A POLIS:
OR KEEP YOUR EYES POINTED ON THE STATE OF THE
WORLD & YOU'LL NEVER HAVE TO CHANGE HOW YOU
BEHAVE TOWARD THE PEOPLE NEAREST YOU

Politics from *πολιτικός*
'of, for, or relating to citizens'
/ amongst others
processes by which groups
always of people
make collective decisions
(like poetry, or quality
like good or bad leaders)
applies to institutions
& fields, even special interest
groups (like poetry)
all segments of society
involving authority & power
like who sings most fairly
or who thinks most rightly
from out the polis

this 'this' of the people.

Property is my poem
given back to me by people
the 'right' to my 're-write'
of a group of people
who have the public trust?
the little, not the main
but when to exercise my right
goes against 'my' people
in the past, present or future
so the growth of my opinion
like the history of knowledge
which is the history of property
is the history of probably
as institutional structure
as protection in numbers
it is exclusionary as anything
it is invisible as I'm in it

the more man becomes knowledgeable
more world he owns,
the more man becomes knowledgeable
more world he owes.

POEM TO BE RECITED AT PROTEST RALLIES WHEN RIOT POLICE IS TWENTY METRES AWAY
UNIVERSAL JENNY

I am ready to think
I am ready to clash

tell me which language you speak
tell which abyss you can bear
I know why I am here
I am because I hate you

I am not being contentious
I am not saying this on purpose
I am not challenging you
that is not my intention

you will hit me
you will hit me
you will hit me

I do not hate you for that

I hate you because

you are simultaneously master and slave-girl
you are full of the teeth I am missing
you believe in the right of the fittest
and when that does not exist you make it up

Come forward come on
Shut my mouth
Smash my face without remorse
Bend me shatter me make me
You can do it you can do it you can do it

THE DEN OF KASDAGLIS
CONSTANTINOS HADZINIKOLAOU

Nikitas falls to the ground and D shoots him point blank in front of passersby tearing open a quick-running flume in his stomach and it's a dry hot lightning bolt that finishes him off. At Patission street he hails a half-full taxi. Syntagma square, he says to the taxi driver. The taxi driver nods at him and D sits in the front seat and then waits to hear the siren of the police car, yet nothing is heard. The taxi arrives at Syntagma, D gets off and crosses the square. He has almost urinated his briefs from the tension. He enters the National Garden, unbuttons his trousers and releases the urine on the grass. The guard sees him and runs towards him and D shoves his hand under his shirt where he has hidden the revolver. The guard backtracks terrified. It is still early, there are no people around, you can hear the airy flutter through the leaves and some birds. D is scared. I will not die today, he mutters. The sweat runs down his back in plaits. He is trembling from head to toe. But will not admit to it. And he is thinking of the birds leaving for the southern shores or crouching inside trees and living in their nests until the cold weather is gone. It is early July now. He phones Nikiforos to ask him for help and Nikiforos the organisation's liaison hangs him out to dry. D does not have enough money on him, and definitely not a passport to go to Patras and take the boat to Italy. He cannot return home because they will be waiting for him there after the tussle: the cops had set up an ambush for them, they shot at Nikitas and D blew one cop's head off. He goes to Nikiforos' house, rings the doorbell, no answer. He jumps into the shaft, climbs up on the external scaffold and breaks down the kitchen door. Nikiforos' flat is empty and D grabs a knife and angrily slashes the sofa. He lies exhausted on the gutted pillows and falls asleep with his mouth open and for a moment the synthetic feathers are stuck high up on the ceiling and then glide down and it's like snow enshrouding him. In the afternoon he goes to the airport. He needs a passport. He hangs around in the toilets and a German tourist who is cruising him approaches him and D speaks to him in German and he remembers the fresh air coming down at an angle from the mountains hitting him on the face when he was studying in Graz and then he hits him and the tourist is screaming like an ox being caned and the blood is spilling out threadlike as if the seams were torn off and in all the stir D escapes once again without having accomplished anything. He is making his way to the centre now. Dusk is drawing near: the atmosphere is still muggy. Near Mitropoleos street he locates a store with glassware and decides to grab the day's collection. He sits and drinks a beer and waits. Let them come, he mutters and grabs tightly in his hand his gun which is cold and becomes warmer only when it fires off and the vibration runs violently across the wrist in parallel to the veins. Shortly before nine he enters the shop and points the gun at the owner. However, the owner reacts and D shoots him in the stomach and then in the head. The owner falls down on the glassware taking down with him the glassware which shatters loudly. The owner is dead, his eyes are rolled back and his tongue pops out and stays there, hanging out. His gums are showing. Some curious passersby have gathered outside the shop. D points the gun at them and the curious onlookers scatter. He kicks at the cash register and grabs the banknotes. He hears the siren, he can hear them now. He hears the police car braking and D goes out into the street and runs. He can hear gunshots behind him and soon he can feel a sting on his back. But he keeps on going. He throws the gun into a storm drain. He goes up Ermou street and loses himself in the crowd. At Syntagma square he gets in a taxi and lies across the back seat. The driver stares at him from the rearview mirror: a young man with tussled hair. I am going to Kypseli, he says. The taxi starts off and D cannot breathe properly, it is as if he is inhaling carbon, exhaling ashes and realises that blood has filled his lungs and the dizziness is making him dream and he is really dreaming he is aboard a raft made of smoked wood on the Lousios river and he is looking at the large deer on the shore drinking calmly water and suddenly he ascertains that they are carrying on their backs other deer, small white deer screeching hoarsely and they are all bloody. The driver is worried. D reassures him. Everything is fine. It is asthma. Are we there yet? We are getting there. He cannot see well. At the entrance of the apartment complex the taxi driver helps him get out of the taxi and then leaves him. He now climbs the steps panting and every so often half-faints. He wishes the cops are waiting for him and that they are tall and that they drag him by the armpits for he is like an animal whose skin has fallen off and it's hanging off the fork formed by the bones. When he reaches his floor, the hallway light goes off. He coughs in the dark. He takes two more steps and reaches the door. He unlocks the door in the dark and enters the flat. It is empty, nobody is there. He staggers as if he were lost and falls on the bed face down and blood starts running from his mouth and nose in lines culminating on his chin. He manages to turn on his back, maybe he will feel better this way and then a lot of blood gushes out of the back of his head, unobstructed, clean and inexhaustible as if there were a red well hidden inside his mattress. D inside the den. Feathers are for birds.

THE CITY THAT DOES NOT EXIST
ALEXIOS MAINAS

Silence with noise.

Earlier tonight at seven
coming down the mausoleum square
I interrupted summer for your sake
at the railing of Stadiou street
where we had almost kissed
to burn the houses down.
The cars would not stop with words alone
the discharged clothes
fell on the scales of the shop window
shattering into dosh,
poverty was branching out, glistening
in the tufts of the teargas
disseminated by the innards of rallying cries
about your sticking to Glasgow this year
to get paid in pounds,
about the beggar on Aeolou street
with the swollen foot
splayed out like a polyp
who stopped pushing his nails

into the base of the fence,
and about the garbage cats
climbing out of bags in the junkyard
painted with hunger,
because I was wandering the streets among the concrete buildings
trying to imitate the smoke
and write dialogues on the walls
where you used to protest with a low voice
that if I had a job
I could kiss you,
and where the scabbed hand of the homeless man
emerges like a match from his cardboard box
squeezing a paper cup with Deutsche marks
from tourists looking among the rabble for the sun
which at that time slips out through the narrows off Ermou street
to buy scorched shoes.

SOUTH (AN EXCERPT)
KATERINA ILIOPOULOU

A most beautiful universe is a pouring out of sweepings at random.
Heraclitus

Passage I

Trapped in the before and after
we cast furtive glances at the mirror
in it our face is hard
already shows marks
Ahead the road,
youth's unblemished face.
Here, together, in the same body.
It didn't leave
it's not a road you take
nor a skein that unwinds to the end
It's a shell which is built from the inside
without seeing the exit
without finding the direction
An unknown intention
unquenched
and the journey is unravelling

not destination
So then let's unravel the stitches.
My grandmother unravelled
a complete man's suit
within a single night
and restitched it from the beginning
from the inside out
That way she doubled its life
from the inside out
It's a two-way route
every instant
every instant multiple
both forward and backward
and even, the same route over and over.
It was no trick. But skilfull craft.
What's more without a craftsman's knowledge
all things are doubly lost.
Both as present and as remembrance.
Let the time well up
the ordeal is the passage
To find a way to pass even through a buttonhole
Not to move ahead but to happen.

Passage II

The landscape disappears
the mountains in the background
a yellow blue dematerialization
the friends' faces given up to sleep
on the back seat
I am driving this moving cradle
that contains us
we are travelling together
twenty years we've looked at one another
companions
in tens of rituals
of ecstasy
of pain
of disappointment
the weight of interpretation
of someone who knows you
What does he know about you?
Unknown
This your unknown meets you in his gaze
the passage point which permits you
to be multiple without knowing the dance steps
the tango that we danced intoxicated and strangers
here travellers-readers-trackers.

Your unknown
the vertigo
of the unknown
that brings you joy
intimate but not familiar
which lets the journey happen
without stop lets the blood flow with force
and the heart beat
and leaves this non-comprehension to the journey.
The journey is this
and the place is this.
Necessity is the boundary
the knowledge, separation;
the certainty of the ephemeral.
Forgetfulness
you are mute and blind in its service
when it happens and extracts
from a body elements, ideas, questions,
skin, tendons.
Oblivion, the source of doubt upon the tongue.
How can you maintain the light there
the quality and randomness of movement,
hesitation and impulse,
agitation.
Flows away

the beauty.
We lost the shadowed details.
Words are always the reverse movement
within desire
which is impossible to fulfill
the wave that ebbs is not the same wave that shot forward.
Here the present leaps in motionless moments
like drops on an automobile's hot hood
recording and loss.
Silence in motion
where present
vanishes as it happens
it passes as it befalls.
I enter into you (homeland)
I travel to you
without names
always distant
always in me pulsates
limitless other
from birth
fatal encounter
affirmation

Translation by John O'Kane

A FLAG IS DOWN ON THE FIELD
TRYFON TOLIDES

At the airport, again. The weather nearly Thanksgiving
gray, but forecast calls for temps to climb into the 70's.
Halloween almost here, midterm elections, football on the monitors,
rules, violence. Waiting in the blue chairs by the gate, my head
tilted up. I'm going away, again, or home, or somewhere
else — it's all of these. From home to home.
The plane is here, fuming, being unloaded still,

back and forth in the nowhere of our days. What if I stayed
in football cider weather, high school games in freezing
cold, Thanksgiving cookies to bring to houses on a wet cold day,
football on the television, appetizers, the day wearing on
to darkness, the drive home, my room?
A kind of comfort. But what when the other home wears on
in some version of this, where I am going?

CIVILISATION'S GOLDEN DAWN: A SLIDE SHOW
CHRISTODOULOS MAKRIS

The navy and army sail the Mediterranean, invading areas as far north as Modern Russia.

Popular singer Yiannis Poulopoulos — open shirt, hairy chest — tickles a young girl.

In the 1830s a new language called katharévousa (meaning pure) was created.

Plaka. Molon Labe. Achilles. Zappeion.

Poustraki finished, you understand? Poustrakia run out. Come kolompichtes, soft ass actors, actresses e assholes ass. Look poutanaki comes your time. D Pull, pull, comes your time. D comes and your police guard the ass after your gamane you gamane the Pakistani man. Sisters torn. Albanian fucking asshole, fucking with Albanian asshole.

Man sitting on a ledge looking moody, stone mountains hanging mid-air behind him.

It's a presidential republic.
A Mazda car. A Carlsberg bag. Picnic on the grass.

Processions leave churches at midnight to re-enact the search for Christ's body.

Riding on the Athens Tram. Happy.

Crisis is a Greek word. Crisis means having people enter parliament who'll bring the country five hundred years back.

Stalagmites, stalactites, navigated by boat.

Albanian refugees are given shelter and jobs.

Feeding pigeons. Isthmus. Amusement park. Some ruins.

Popular singer Kostas Karalis on a personally signed promotional postcard.

The Ancient Greek phrase μολὼν λαβέ (molṑn labé; reconstructed Ancient Greek pronunciation [mo'lɔːn la'be]; Modern Greek pronunciation [mo'lon la've]) means "Come and take them". It is a classical expression of defiance reportedly spoken by King Leonidas I in response to the Persian army's demand that the Spartans surrender their weapons at the Battle of Thermopylae. It is an exemplary use of a laconic phrase.

Churches. Monuments. Moving escalators.

The system of dowries is no longer practiced.

Boy poses alongside tsolias (meaning presidential guard).

Would you call a male politician throwing a glass of water and a right-left-right hook at female members of parliament on live TV macho, or funny?

The unknown soldier.

Laughing so hard she ends up in hospital.

Boy sitting on a ledge, stone mountains hanging mid-air behind him, looking down.

Food and hospitality are important to culture.

Thessaloniki: a goalkeeper lunge, an open window, broken glass, a deep cut above the left eye, to hospital for stitches.
All packed up.

City dwellers participate in exercise, go to parks and walk their dogs. In rural areas people visit each other and host parties.

Out of focus at proscenium of amphitheatre. Man tossing coin demonstrates unbelievable acoustics.

Literally: "number". The Huffington Post translates it as "circus act". My dictionary says "odd character". None is individually adequate.

At the border with Yugoslavia. Bird, nationality unknown, shits on boy's head. A lucky omen.

Who's this striking young couple?

Ochi (meaning No) Day celebrates pride.

Impressed by the large flower clock at Patras.

More ruins.

Folk dances range from the festive and happy to the serious and solemn.

Poystraki finish, got it? Run the poystrakia. ADE kwlompichtes, assholes, kwloy actors with actors of kwloy assholes. Look at poytanaki, your time is coming. Trava Trava, comes the time. PE and comes your police guard the kwlarakia after your your gamane gamane which Pakistanis eh. Xeskismenes sisters. Gamimenes Albanian kwlotrypides Albanian gamimenes, kwlotrypides.

Popular singer Stamatis Kokotas in a smart suit smiles for the camera.

Ascending the stairs to the airplane. (Hold on, wasn't this trip taken by boat? Didn't a suitcase fall off the roof of the car while driving out of Piraeus, clothes scattered all over the highway?)

Ninety-eight per cent of the population belongs to the Orthodox Church. Muslims, Roman Catholics, Protestants and Jews account for two per cent.

Watching a parade of guards. The infantry. The navy.

An olive tree at Olympia, woman posing at the start line, children already racing.

Do we deserve this?

Boy clutching promotional postcard stands alongside another boy, a popular act in a travelling circus from Russia.

'I want to gatecrash history'

>

ACCELERATION

MIGRATORY BIRDS
KIRIAKOS SIFILTZOGLOU

the country is suffering
from viral hemorrhagic fever

a weak spring
and a headache
hospitality manifest as a rash

a nymph of ominous times
coming from Senegal
slept at Antikythera

sleep might as well be
a defence against wayfaring

the environment
is not that natural
immature mammals
breastfeed immaturely

so what if we are
the best hosts

the blame
will always fall
on a
  red
   breast

THE MINOANS
THANASIS TRIARIDIS

The Minoans assemble every month at the port
to see the new sacrificial victims arriving like clockwork:
the young men and the young women who are to be devoured by the
             Minotaur.
And the people watch silently the decked out prisoners,
some mumble through their teeth "What a shame these poor
children".

And everybody on the island knows
that there is absolutely no monster inside the Labyrinth,
that the Minotaur is a crude fairytale.
That Pasiphaë is bent on eating virgin meat
and Minoas devised the story with the monster
so that the allies would not start grumbling,
so that the people would not be alarmed — people get alarmed with
things like this…

This is what The Minoans did:
they watched the sacrificial victims arrive every time,
and then they dispersed quietly, with some sadness of course,
but also with considerable relief that foreign flesh, and not
             their own,
fed Pasiphaë's madness.

EKURHULENI

ELENI PHILIPPOU

We cannot wash the graves
in Germiston cemetery.
The dust builds
on the black granite,
obscures the names
Kyriakoula and Peter.
The municipality has cut the water
because people
came from the townships
with their cracked plastic buckets
and their children,
in shweshwe skirts
and dull stars of Zion
pinned to loose breast pockets.
Now there are taps without handles
and tattered tape
just to remind these living
to return to their homes
of corrugated iron
and soil-encrusted paper,
for even among the dead
they will find no relief.

HRAM[1]
MARIOS CHATZIPROKOPIOU

Little azure girl that twenty years afore
you were watering with milk your grandfather's bedding, swishing
grandchild

Barren you now sweat to saddle yourself with them, a tourist
childless
disowned
offspring
                                                              with money
of unknown origin self
creating. Glass-like skin longing to be scratched

Website: "Easter at the village"

(-Does Resurrection ever sound
in the hecatombs of the chests?

---

[1] *hram*: wool-cotton bedding [...] Agiasos, Lesbos [...] idiom [...] Turkish ihram [...] ihrām ارح arabic [...] garment [...] faithful to Islam [...] psychological condition [...] pilgrimage, hajj حج [...] harām حار [...] holy/sinful [...] Etym. arab root *h-r-m*: holy/ forbidden [...] Modern Gr. χράμι (bedding), χαράμι (wasted attempt), χαραμίζω (squander), χαραμής (thief), χαρέμι (harem) [...]

—For certain, daughter of mine, for certain)

The beddings that raised you, wares
you haggle over with foxes rabbit-sisters
bishops brothers scions and acquired
telesalesmen of the family house.

The years that corroded you, pixels
online pics and you grope around in the hope of finding
and (re)claiming with a credit card number
the mark of shame that bore you.

PHOBOS-GRUNT[1]
IORDANIS PAPADOPOULOS

We never got this close to Phobos before, exceeding every prediction made by scientists in Laputa.

"...a few hours later we located a blurry object. No sooner had we been able to ascertain its position than the fog from the river stopped us."

Something is not right with Phobos. Its density is distinctly smaller than that of marble, but even then its use in the production of pillows is bizzare. It is being cut and sewn clumsily, like a pattern of readymade clothing with a compass and quadrant. Despite all that it is being worn unwisely and Gulliver looks on mystified.

"...The sky cleared after a storm. The atmosphere was glaring and unstable rendering the object invisible even though we knew it was so close."

The degree of reflection of light on it is as minimal as the possibilities of the cucumbers of Laputa to emit solar rays. Since its premature fictional discovery in 1700 it rises and sets in points which are by

---

[1] Phobos is the larger and closer of the two natural satellites of Mars and was discovered by astronomer Asaph Hall on August 18, 1877. Geological features on Phobos are named after people and places from Jonathan Swift's *Gulliver's Travels*.

default an oxymoron. In a potential contact with it, disembodiment is foreseen.

"On the 16th of August it was detected on the opposite side, it was moving and it was near its greatest elongation. Until that point we had never told anyone anything."

The scenario to be used as the basis of observation of the Red Planet is under serious consideration (the alternative scenario of revealing political conspiracies through the analysis of suspects' faeces was refuted as a figment of Gulliver's imagination). Until then and under its constant, hefty shadow, as retaliation to our attempts to fight back and extract its secrets, we will take high resolution pictures using flashlight.

"The observations of the 17th and the 18th of August confirmed beyond any doubt the nature of that body and its discovery was disclosed publicly."

Gulliver professes his wish to return home.

I DID NOT COME FROM THE WOODS
CONSTANTINOS HADZINIKOLAOU

I did not come from the woods.
I was born here.
I never strayed far from my house.
My parents were nice (but idiots).
They still give me a plate of food.
Time passes by quickly after all
and I never got the chance to do enough.
I did not make money
I did not fall in love
I did not live a lot.
A few years ago
a woman gave birth to my child.
The woman left.
I am now raising my son on my own
but I have nothing to offer him.
I am trying to teach him
to be fair and to be imaginative
(piddly stuff really) but
I am not a good teacher.
I like to read and to walk.
Some times I feel dirty while other times clean.
When the animals arrive I will give myself to them.

THE HISTORY OF TOO MUCH
ADRIANNE KALFOPOULOU

There is too much here, the sapphire, the thistle,
the oregano blooms in June, everything extravagant —
the rich peat of what decays, the ruins that don't decay,
these especially are too much, the temples and statues
in their stark marble glow, that simplicity which is not simple at all.
This sheen of time, the wear of wars, the famine years
of Occupation, lucent as the columns standing stoic, Doric —
their weight has whittled the people: the weight of that antiquity,
of those stones, the grandeur and pride — too much
in this moment, this present crushed by the violence,
the result of living with beheaded gods, and maimed, still
beautiful torsos, the muscled limbs in chipped robes.
They plague our dreams, what was once achieved is now
incomplete, these pieces of the golden age aging
in the midst of traffic, too much, the yelling and honking,
the protests in the middle of everything — people are impatient —
how can anyone be patient, overwhelmed as they are.
Even the oregano's thick perfume, the sapphire sea,
remind people of extravagant loves and sacrifice, while here,
now, ghosts live on as gods and their impossibility.

SMALL POEM IN MEMORY OF SUICIDE VICTIM DIMITRIS CHRISTOULAS, RETIRED PHARMACIST

STAMATIS POLENAKIS

History has taught us nothing
and the winter of the great hunger is forthcoming
in this blind police state
in this global republic of Salo
where our worst nightmares are slowly taking shape.
Even the terrible cry even the gunshot
Of that despairing suicide
even though it should have broken all the windows
And rocked this crumbling world
To its very core
It was not heard beyond the tiny Syntagma square
Because order rules once again in Berlin
And the city band and all the security units
Parade underneath bolted shut dark windows
In the empty streets of this deeply defeated country.
And this is how it ended the third year
Of this terrible war recounted by Thucydides.

VIOLENT MAGNESIUM
HOLOBIOTIC STUDY OF REPETITION
DIMITRIS ALLOS

*The greater
the unexpressed a man
carries inside him
all the more
he belongs to this world.
Metrephysics A, 7*

*...I returned the symbol
to the word; I followed, the
palpable method of sorrow
Metrephysics A, 11*

*The poet when he writes
does not justify poetry
he sets it free
Metrephysics B, 19*

*Dedicated
to whoever is being identified*

This winter the wire
will run through many souls

*

The suspension points of the previous poem
I have made them into thick pellet
for my grandfather's old front-loading rifle
at the crack of dawn   on the tip of our feet   circum-
scribing   all the squarings of death
I went out to hunt
                    the blind   boar of the mysteries
it was only yesterday when we mourned yet another dead
better off on my own — I said

[...]
A number of years later
something wild within me was looking for a stronghold
(a lot of blood was built here)
I wandered across the violent magnesium of love
   I saw the great vultures
      I concealed leniencies
I saw words getting stranded in existence
between the easy solution and the hope
I was left with a defect in walking
by these Clashing Rocks
   I divided the uniformity of every truth

and their dual number
schizophrenia with welding
          [...]
a number of years later
   with asphalt sangfroid
   I am considering leaving this foreign land
the Tripoli which I loved
          many burrows were opened here
                many handguns I fostered in here

[C]
The whip of distance
          hits whoever holds it
                [...]
do not play roulette with my words

[C]
Motionless you admire speed

the absolute horror to pass by
whatever time entrusted you with
                [...]
be careful how you handle words

they conceal incidents

*

N.G.

Let them

[I wanted to tell you "don't be afraid"
   sole benefactor responsible
for whatever happens to you   is yourself
   this is an indestructible armour
if you know   how to wear it
   — but these things   I had told you about before —
I held your upper arm tightly so that you would understand
   that courage   is not a word
it is a sea laden   with shores
broken metal plates — look in the
old dictionaries as well   to see   how close
you were —   an astute error
is more valuable than its truth
   do not repeat yourself when
you repeat — let them — you will set up
a feeble tent (there is nothing wrong with ten-
ts) at some point   you will wheeze   with
force and the wind will take them away — this stuff

here   (−twice); this is my shattering

    after an innocence
the gaze   grows rancid in the eyes −let them−
she will get a whiff of you − (you know who)] but all of this
    we had talked about   so many times

I was looking for the handkerchief for a while now
(and with a small hesitation)
I restricted myself to cleaning my nails
−nevertheless with grave propriety

AGEMISTI
BARNABY TIDEMAN

young serbian assasin// shee at high water//
as if how many girls and their hairstyles/
your fulsome/ and taking fulinarum/
Pyramids, arches and obelisks are melting pillars of

snow. The frigid zone/ among the victors weary of their success/
our meg/ excites angels to our help/ like a judge on his circuit/

at one more percentage point just interview yourself.
Batteried hanging isn't as possible//
though she were still dockt in the sands, almost foure foot,
pretty sure,

our ancestors,

I have ever used in my life. The wind in furs,
the dream was wonky; learing sounds, shee in a denim jacket, falling
off,

and those effective? Of whom holidays? Wine-like spirits and
heaving

swimsuit? We argue that the Dirac-Born-Infeld (DBI) action
coupled to a tachyon? Brown and maturing
managerial Briton and his foreign broad, placed nowhere what,

our dreamt reflection gravelled. Ah so long
but that truer violet / Ah come by,
/ recall my cycle down Fulham road,
matt reflections where churches downed

And so she answered Sarah, until blonde and sheer
workers at the railhead
creak to the gasworks turntable: chalky and thin,
'This was an idea waiting for a person'
; oil for the hinge. I was dead broke, waiting on fifty notes,
she came against me as her friends carried her past
with black curls and a kiss for me and no-one,
a crushed rose. I slept over reservoirs,
muzzles at the sky, a week's sustenance
laid on England's earthy eye.

*

Nights holds faintly on the hillside,
stark spotlights cut with rock;
but in the grain store, mound of bricks,

the zero grinding stops:
how the air processes volatile, scrapes against his neck.
How real, from the pre-fab above London where they lectured
like a tropical disease
at the end of a suburban garden, to the Hellenic alluvial plains
hanging at altitude, cracked rain and creased sealight
fold in the giant panning lifted to northcoast stiff
and floored to a rug at the south,
searching for examples most ready, most prospective,
most edged with the desire to be joined —

Wearing darkly ambyr horn rim
and heavy checked shirts, blackwatch tartan
of loose girth/ Moves in./ Like a fish out of water
shivering with thirst: there is a certain revenge
of good will and there is only one precise serpentine line
that I call the line of grace;
a certain guilt of the autobiographical turn, jobless mob
leave home at 6 as normal
fill Attika motorway with empty tanks/ But there is a smile
hanging in the night
and filled with smoke — distant ink,
empty ranks,
barbershop of square cut glass
downed at oceanic sunset. There is a replacement

to which he'll return. Co-authors,
those white terrorists/ hacking and wired beards
/sweating rolls in filthy apartments, parts of the chase
harsh digital whispering/ sick mopeds portwards
The days are so forgiving. To you they are easily warmed.
A fish market on an urban island
bad winter and twanging same,
a palace language/ the landscape like the frame
of an ancient bird flying everywhere/
the last record of the civilisation, tablets
recording the dispatch of coast watchers
hilltop palaces burnt by a subservient class
that had always been there
or the riddled sea peoples
//

MAID OF ATHENS: που μένετε;
skins dwells like honey at the edges of features of the face
glowing brown, peach and pink the nose speleothem
liquid turns into black eyebrows/ pink lips on light brown skin,
eyes a gasping mineral, blue and green black dust at the corners
Sweet Brycea, up for walking —
bathed bright in the soft songs
along the evening city, the scent of wild flowers
like a veil from the hills —
down the promenades in fresh clothes?

/ diagonally through the Bosphorous, the marble sea, Crimea,
savage run for earnings and self respect
or criminal trading of petrol necessities & motorbikes
washed up at the skirts of wrecks, diagonal liners
penal islands, string of bitter lakes
fabled armies swallowed/ commissioned burglaries/
or layer of charred earth
flinging cigarettes into the cars behind, this happened over
and over

opening the city//her worn jewels, smoke washing through beaded
curtains,
batted eyelashes, watch spats hour,
oxblood English brogues, socks striped not throwaway, καστανά
hair
done up in teeterful shape, might've been born black but
ten weird things about Mediterranean streets
apparently want 'uncorporate information'
at 12 she has planned to attend CONCENTRATION AGAIN THE
PET SHOP ATHENS

straw boaters raised to the sun, sudary dragged across her wails
he wants to do away with prepositions and conjunctions
pacing flicked pages pays the garage's rent/ palm trees thrash
against

condominiums/ with juvenile insects in their heads, we refuse to
consent
to anything that can keep what you called system we battlefield. Oh
at night,
to walk alone through the shells of phonecalls
and the mysteries of scent, she is nervous
about the silence of what else

/turn it on unrequited, Make of your Prayers one sweet Sacrifice
to starve pronouns to death, sink them into the word,
awakening to the art of portraiture alone in a comprehensive school
marine ashes fetch length /the depreciation of my good name, my
character and my aims/

empty-headed-high by the rusted steamtrain/ a smog that insulted
people
skulking inevitably, ex-motor shop becomes fortress of solitude/
with metal sign in purist Greek
\lunch made by basement women, Byzantine queens,
really the hours circular frustrate his work
decorations dripping from the shelf; reaching for the thick book
that leaves a white shadow on the concrete ledge

the tendons hesitate —
frame unsure of itself —

throat is a wreck, grinding around the fresh water
paused in your self. He who has few Things to desire cannot have
many to fear. Hound lolls with friends and runs out of hills
wet smoke trailing stunned manus
eyes blood hooded, short ears, traction on growl paws scattered
haphazard drill:
the storm streams out of its blister
into a second event; crumpled pediment of heaven
and how to manage the vertex distantly spewing rain
high tail, skidding health with wooden skull/
knows when a bark has done all it has to tell; sickness to the heart
with prejudices and false first impressions that re-emerge
waiting for the next line in the queue to fill, he must name
everything
read all books again, avoid mistakes,
droplets owed to the callers falling sideways
onto the croft, chosen by lot, the falling, isolated monument

won't be back for weeks, lost cause with full engagement of life, the
women await
movement from the hills, oxen teams called in from the Argolid

and with wedding-song in clans local
firing the caged tympanum /stalled pensions /eyes blue
has engineer on hull drum,

bruised palms hesitant crouching, Pharisaic donations,
Japanese ports and the rush, the quiet,

the furthest to sea towards dusk. Blackout for coastal Brooklyn:
emigrant of self-sabotaging alpine unit
stares at the prolonged fragments
moving against New York.
Limestone moves in, stokes agèd weapon
woman with thoughtful shadow warily enters doorway, mammoth
inhalation
of nekyia tired from air pressure and atlantic gyres
crouched under black mask of the winds before
lit up and vitrified fort.
Dark man in handcuffs pulled in, Trojans vegetating in the dusk
her face darkened with a smile every time we met
the bells sounding like tin, beaten domes and panels of sealed
santouri
drowned on the mainland
beyond the waves; beyond this plain and the line of golden towns
blistering the lips of blinking pelago; a bowl of apricots ringing
in the fridge and the statues of a submerged town spear through the
shoal
who cheer and cry at the velvet edges of dowry/ cows of stone
paid pretty dearly for my fourpenny piece,
it was a trauma I would cherish until it was not raw.

THE TABLE
ORFEAS APERGIS

The door is half-open and you can see in it
the waters of the wood
and on it some light, albeit somewhat intense,
perhaps from the bare garden or the incandescent
lamp,
that one however cannot make out.
Next to it the drawer with the silverware, round,
sculpted with bizarre creatures,
desirous, namely satyrs and nymphs and small
animals for slaughter
with swollen livers, assured, unctuous,
as if they were being prepared for sacrifice,
ready,
immotile,
caught inside the intricacies of the cedar wood.
Ahead,
underneath the lamp,
or in the light of the garden,
it floats, you would think, the table,
it levitates inside its whiteness, surrounded
by its shadows in purple,

its legs never showing,

that is to say without any apparent holdings, worthwhile,

like a white tablet,

like a wax

tablet

engraved with the laws of fruits,

the possession of food

and the burnt offering.

But no,

it is probably morning,

a morning with not too much light, apocalyptic,

miserable,

with a reddish light,

falling on the spots of colour

as if it were spotty,

papulous destiny,

like a meaning deathly and frightening.

A girl with glasses sits on one end

of the table,

fiddles with a small pomegranate,

picks its seeds off,

it is their season and soon there will be no more,

but for a little while the girl can rejoice in them,

those crimson little seeds

she crunches inbetween her dogteeth

and her molars.
The pomegranates are placed on the table,
on the white surface discreetly smelling
of her chlorine,
inside a big bowl
made of delicate porcelain
with a footrest,
which from up close is revealed to be decorated
with six crotcheted branches of
an almond tree,
with the corresponding sepals and flowers,
and with some deterioration around its edges,
a bit worn by use,
by the repetition of the same food
of this selfsame season
of spring, that runs in circles
even more infrequently,
but existent,
so that they might justify the damage
and the restitution
and the reinstatement,
as a ritual,
whenever the pomegranates mature
and break open
and their blood pours plenty,

thick, as if it were part of an animal writhing struck
by savage ire, human-like,
part of a sacrifice,
when everybody is substituted
by their animal.

On the table,
it goes on,
it is also the bread that is inescapable,
cut in slices,
from pure semolina,
a bit burnt,
with the knife next to it
for spreading butter
glistening like gold from the verdigris,
for the local priest has to eat too,
the stinking priest with his privates
the lewd ones, the unearned ones,
oh they hang like gongs and the girl sees them
with those glances of absolute intent,
with her eyes resembling tassels in the shape of a pomegranate,
drowned in the blood of lust,
this is how the priest eats the butter pears
when he beseeches and remembers
his origin, from Aaron,

and walks on his bed.

Twelve slices is how large the bread is
if you have not yet understood it,
kneaded from pure orthodoxies,
a cut made holiest from all the sacrifices
that are carried out with fire
and seed
and with a black wine libation.

This is how we commune with what we are made of
and this is how we sit,
on the right of the girl
and fill the lovely orchard
with the pomegranates and the grain of wheat,
bread and blood
and the final, fatal parenthesis
where we realise that
the table is made of acacia
and that that her glasses have slightly cracked
and furthermore the surface is not holding well,
that it's missing legs
that the carpenter has gone under
and that all the money is gone
and the trees are no longer cut

but turn into something like gallows

and that we drowned you guys
inside a borrowed conviction
and inside a devious atonement,
oh what a terrible and austere construct,
oh what an official happiness,
the crippled table
is made of boards, hollow on the inside,
deplorable board,
concave and overly gilded,
like the mercy seat with the two angels
and the horns on four corners.

Underneath the table,
— time cannot withstand allegory —
you can see the inside altar,
the boilers,
the shovels, the grills
and the large fleshhook with the fresh fat,
all made of brass,
vulgar.

HOMELESS (ROOF-LESS)
PHOEBE GIANNISI

this morning inside the room
we found a bird flapping its wings
imprisoned with the window wide open
it would begin gathering speed to fly
then hit the ceiling
the square room did not allow for flight
nests
roofless houses of birds
each one with his own sky
each one with his own freedom.

Translated by Aggelos Sakkis

PETROL STATION UNDER THE MERCILESS SUN IN THE MIDDLE OF NOWHERE

PATRICIA KOLAITI

The things that must be done at a petrol station are endless. If you
had ever lived at a petrol station you would know. First you have to
meticulously wash the thick dust off objects which will be inevitably
buried under even thicker dust. To take a thing from here and take
it there where you have taken it a thousand times before and from
there to here and from here to there. To tighten a bolt with care.
And when you are done with all of these,
to sit
on that chair which always creaks under your weight
and to look at
the endless straight line
from which nothing ever came.

THE NEW SYMMETRY
NIKOS ERINAKIS

The concept of the cycle troubles me still

I am in fear of everything that was created over the centuries
Their balance suggests decay

What happened to the sun and it ended up like that

I feel the great change approaching
I will sleep until Spring
The words of memory will accompany me

I count the dead things on the path I travel
I lean on ancient moments

When are we going to find ourselves again on this side of death?

At the point where the circle opens
Behind time

I repel ghosts
I experience the world as something on the edge

The only thing that wears me out
Is the stillness of truth
I still believe in beauty

Myth re-enters
In the rhythm of what has no measure
It needs no verification

Even though it is still raining down on us

Most kings end up with a severed head

Every number has more than meaning
The allure of prison
Every impulse will be forgiven
We are part of certain bets between saints

We are part of the reflection
While she is not part of us

And it is still pouring down on us

Not will
But the need for will
A different pleasure

An economy of desire

The reproduction of death
If the wind wants to sing it
It will go even through bones to make it happen

It is a fact that pain is heard always louder than pleasure

Uncanny sound; cease

I am under the impression that time and space are no longer
The one and the same
Childhood amnesia
The privilege of the blind
A noble obligation
Or rather a womb of fear

Ultimately it is harder to breathe
Than what I believed when I was born

Stop listening to the voices
Listen to the voice
With no equality
Or proportion of measures

Every man a little before he dies
Wishes he were a woman

The concept of opposition is a trap
The bipolarity of our thinking is to blame
Parallel roads must be discovered

The problem is symbolic

And it's not the endless outside that scares me
But the endless inside

I have no more than a life
And scattered dreams from previous lives to offer

But it is at the altitude of dreams where the battle takes place

I am with no one and this means I am with the majority

It's the new symmetry

We know nothing but we will not retreat yet
Because nothingness has been uttered
And the time for something has come
A while has passed but not time

Paradise has not yer been defined
Perhaps only innocence
So many gods we have invented we are bound to find the one

And if only death and nothingness are the only things left for us
Then in death and nothingness we shall find hope

We have always had the sun with us
And from what I see the sun is still here

IN HEAVEN EVERYTHING IS FINE
KATERINA ILIOPOULOU

A small room
A window in front of the sea
The bare landscape, the geological unfoldings
You circumscribe them with your stare countless times every day
The body follows them
And a small window across the bed
Black hills at night
And crickets

We came here to be on our own
But we are not
We are not on our own
There are rooms carved on the rock
There is a town.
When we lie there for hours on end,
On the stone cradles
We match our bodies to theirs
Sometimes inside the salt nests
We let their hands burn the palm of our hands.
We drape ourselves with the heavy cloak of their breathing in the
heat

It is summer you tend to believe that
Clouds and the green grass will never return
The small rock flowers.
We are trapped inside a child's drawing
Yellow and blue
Drawn with thick strokes everywhere
And ourselves two points
In a prehistoric room
We burn with them on the rocks
Like immortals
One on top of the other
One for the other
One inside the other
One against the other
The small rock temple in the heartland
An eye completely exposed
From there you can really weep
Looking at the sky

You are so alone when you sleep
You are never alone when you sleep
(Within reach)
Your body is never
Outside the reach of my hand

And words

A thread

we pull one from the mouth of the other

Building a permeable edifice.

Thus when we are together

We find ourselves simultaneously inside and outside the world.

Words are a means of survival

Inside the multiplicity

As if the future existed

Simulation of Paradise

Even the greatest ebullience

Leaves us naked

Exhausted

Lost

"No more stars and sky

Please, let's turn the light on so that I can read".

THE CHAOS
KONSTANTINOS PAPACHARALAMPOS

of   chaos   Ch   Ch   ch   cha   ha

chaos Here with the   Chaos Ch a   ha   cha   And

believe a —   —   nothing one Chaos   which speaks as if it were nothing

a   aa   a   a   in   Your dreams

o   Ch s   o   and all of it ch   ch   Chaos Ch   Ch

— the   a   ch   Don't   You Hear puts on a

Ch   if   you hear   Ch

don't you hear — don't you see   the morning is   the hour is

the body   now is   the dream   and naked it is

there it is   chaos   simultaneous:

chaos is   the order   order is   chaos

— you now believe   and you laugh ha   ha-ha

and it isn't laughing — h h h ahah   a   h a   a H a

DAYS TO
UNIVERSAL JENNY

Get out screaming in a shrilly voice
Skin the arm bearing the "listen to me" tattoo
Erase the penalty as if it were a word
Awaken the quandary
Stand far back, on the right of the sewer
Summarise the contradictions of the fifteenth minute of escape
Remind that you are crying
Beg that you are capable of
Make aware that you are willing to
Insist that you are laughing
Round up the weaknesses
Make the dress fit the second back
Be subjected to the mirror with the white fault lines
Travel imperceptibly
Repeat "my fears"
Counter the onslaught
Be replaced
Imply antinomies
Divide the illogical
Make goods contemporary
Eat coherently

Push over the cliff whatever's moving your way
Neutralise the verb "to shock"
Steal with the consciousness of uncoordinated struggle
Escort instability to the events
Respond to the culprits
Draw courage from zero
Materialise stasis constructively
Elate without restraint
Converse with your female dead
Indicate forgiveness
Structure regret
Change through voluntarism
Expand meaninglessly
Legislate against the recent past
Claim without mashalling together
Neglect without emotional pain
Refract ineffectively and fruitlessly
Fire manageable sorrows
Disagree with visible wounds
Re-articulate on the basis of a singular criterion
Suspect the timeless
Bury by accident
Be possibly insurgent
Systematise untameness
Detract

THE INVISIBLE MAN OR PLAN FOR A REVOLUTION
YIANNIS STIGGAS

First of all, it's not just one person
it's a lot of peoplé
who have for years been flashing like indicator lights
in the hope that some Christian person
or at the very least, a crane
from roadside assistance
might see them.
Until one night — snap —
"the fuse blows"
and this, it turns out, is how
the dogcatcher finally finds them in the dark
and christens them in the cold.
This is why the motto is hereby
allocated as a locker
for them to take off
their shoes
their socks, their Mondays,
their vests,
their Tuesdays, their watches, hats,
briefs, goggles and their faith
to dry

and everyone to rush out stark bollock naked

and de jure

Out

To —

It's the first time
I see a horizon
                getting flayed
(of its own accord)
from top to bottom

In a matter of minutes
Athens follows.

Whoever dares
Should go round them up.

BIOGRAPHICAL NOTES

Dimitris Allos has published two poetry collections. His poems have been included in various anthologies.

Orfeas Apergis has been publishing in Greek literary journals since 2006. His collected poems, *Y* (Patakis), appeared in 2011. In 2013, he was poet-in-residence at King's College, London, Department of Classics and Hellenic Studies, and visiting poet at the University of Barcelona, Department of Sociology.

Vassilis Amanatidis has published seven collections, from *Dormitory: Nine nocturnal parables* (Entefktirio, Thessaloniki 1999) to *m_otherpoem: mono logue* (Nefeli, 2014). He has published two collections of short stories: *Don't eat me* (Kastaniotis, Athens 2005) and *Charybdis' Dog* (Kastaniotis 2008). Two of his plays have been staged in Thessaloniki and he is also an acclaimed performer of his own works.

Marios Chatziprokopiou's writing has appeared in *Enteyktirion, [FRMK], The Books' Journal* and *Bibliotheque*. His performances have been presented in venues and festivals such as: *MOstra LAtinoamericana de Performances Urbanas* (Salvador de Bahia 2010), *Perfor1* (São Paulo 2010), *Political Performance* (Belgrade 2011), *Macedonian Museum of Contemporary Art* (Thessaloniki 2012) and *Dimitria* (Thessaloniki 2015).

Theodoros Chiotis writes poetry and code poetry in Greek and English. His work has appeared in print and online magazines and anthologies in Greece, the UK, the US, Australia, Sweden, Turkey and Croatia. He has translated contemporary British and American poets and continental philosophy into Greek and Aristophanes into English. His debut collection in Greek will be published in early 2016.

Emily Critchley is the author of several poetry collections (with Arehouse, Bad press, Dusie, Oystercatcher, Torque, Holdfire, Corrupt and Intercapillary presses) and a selected writing: *Love / All That / & OK* (Penned in the Margins, 2011). She teaches English and Creative Writing at the University of Greenwich.

Yiannis Doukas' books are: *The world as I came and found it* (Kedros, 2001), *On inner borders* (Polis, 2011, Debut poetry collection prize of the Diavazo magazine) and *The Stendhal syndrome* (Polis, 2013, G. Athanas prize of the Academy of Athens).

Nikos Erinakis has published two poetry books *Soon everything will be burning and will lit up your eyes* (Roes, 2009) and *In between where the shadow falls* (Gavrielidis, 2013), as well as a translation of poems by Georg Trakl and passages by Martin Heidegger: *Dark love of a wild generation* (Gavrielides, 2011). His essays and poems have been included in anthologies and journals and have been translated into five languages.

Phoebe Giannisi has published five books of poetry: *Sea Urchins* (1995), *Ramazan* (1997), *Loops* (2005), *Homerica* (2009), *Tettix* (2012). She has translated Ancient lyric poetry and work by Hélène Cixous, Valery Coulton, Barbara Koehler, Joseph Mosconi, André Pieyre de Mandiargues, Jesper Svenbro. In 2012 she presented the poetic audiovisual installation *Tettix* at the National Museum of Contemporary Art in Athens.

Constantinos Hadzinikolaou is a filmmaker and writer. His pamphlet *Notes from the Mountains* was published in 2009. His work *Antidog* was performed in the form of directed readings at the Greek National Theatre in 2009.

Katerina Iliopoulou is a poet and translator who has published four books of poetry. Her most recent is *Every place, once, and completely* (2015). Her translations include the work of, Sylvia Plath (*Ariel: the restored edition*), Mina Loy, Robert Hass and Ted Hughes. She is co-editor of greekpoetrynow.com and editor in chief of ΦΡΜΚ (*pharmakon*), a biannual journal, on poetry, poetics, and the visual arts.

Panayotis Ioannidis has published two books of poems, *The Lifesaver* (2008) and *Uncovered* (2013), as well as translations of poems by Robert Creeley, Thom Gunn, David Harsent, Seamus Heaney and others. Translations of his poems have appeared in *Poetry London*, *Hotel Amerika* and *Drunken Boat*. He is poetry editor for *The Books' Journal*; on the editorial board of ΦΡΜΚ (*pharmakon*); and founder-curator of the monthly poetry reading, Words (can) do it. His forthcoming poetry book is *Poland*.

D.I. (Dimitra Ioannou) is based in Athens. She experiments with new narrative or anti-narrative forms in various media. She is the founder and editor of the literary and art journal a glimpse of, and the author of the novella *Soya Sea* (Futura, 2008).

Adrianne Kalfopoulou is the author of two collections of poetry and several chapbooks, most recently *Passion Maps* (2009). A book of essays, *Ruin, Essays in Exilic Living* (2014) engages with political and personal crisis-moments during Greece's austerity years, as it is in conversation with wider discussions of mind, place, and gender in late capitalism. The poems included here are part of a manuscript in progress.

Patricia Kolaiti was born in Athens and raised in Aigina. Her debut collection *Celesteia* (Nefeli, 2007) was nominated for the 2008 Diavazo First Book Award. Her work has been translated into English and Dutch and included in journals, anthologies and online platforms. The poems included here come from her forthcoming collection *The Lithopedion (Stonebaby)*. Patricia is an emerging philosopher of literature and art.

Dimitra Kotoula's debut collection *Three Notes for Music* was published in 2004. She has translated Jorie Graham, Louise Gluck and Sharon Olds. Her poems, essays and translations have been presented at poetry festivals in Europe and published online and in literary journals and anthologies in Greece and abroad. Her poetry has been translated, amongst others, by Fiona Shaw, David Connolly, A.E. Stallings, Jacques Bouchard, Ulf Stolterfoht, Michaela Prinzinger and Vladimir Bošković.

Alexios Mainas has published two books: *The content of the remainder* (Gavrielides, 2011, nominated for the State Award for debut author, for the Diavazo Debut Author Award, and a prize winner at the Poetry Symposium at the University of Patras in 2012); and *Occam's Razor* (Mikri Arktos 2014). He edited a German translation of the poems of C.P. Cavafy (Romiosini 2009). He is currently translating Cavafy for a Swiss publishing house. His poems have been translated into German, English and French.

Christodoulos Makris was born in Nicosia and has lived and worked in Manchester, London and, since 2001, Dublin. His most recent book is *The Architecture of Chance* (Wurm Press, 2015). He co-edited the bilingual exchange anthology *Centrifugal: Contemporary Poetry of Guadalajara and Dublin* (EBL-Cielo Abierto/Conaculta, 2014). His curatorial projects include the tour Yes But Are We Enemies. He is poetry editor of gorse journal.

Sophie Mayer's most recent collection *(O)* (Arc, 2015) is a communion with Artemis through Katniss and Pussy Riot. She is the co-editor of *Catechism: Poems for Pussy Riot, Binders Full of Women* and *Glitter is a Gender*, with Sarah Crewe; they also collaborated on *signs of the sistership* (KFS, 2013). She is a feminist film activist @tr0ublemayer (Twitter) and @PoliticalAnimals (Tumblr).

Stergios Mitas was born in Thessaloniki in 1980. He has published the poetry collection *Natural History of Theatres in Verse* (Mikri Arktos, 2013). He is a Lecturer at the Law School of the University of Nicosia.

Eftychia Panayiotou has published *the great gardener* (Koinonia ton (de)katon, 2007), *Black Moralina* (Kedros, 2010) and *Dancers* (Kedros, 2014). *Black Moralina* won third prize for the collection by a new poet at the Poetry Symposium, was nominated for the Cyprus State Poetry Award and the Diavazo Poetry Award. Her work has been translated into various European languages. She translated Anne Sexton's *Love Poems* (Melani, 2010). She co-ordinates the poetry workshop at To Spirto.

Konstantinos Papacharalampos' debut poetry project, *K – On* (Entefktirio), appeared in 2011. His poems have been translated into German, presented at the 1st Festival of New Writers in Athens, performed in the play *One minute of silence,* and installed in the contemporary visual arts festival Action Field Kodra in Thessaloniki. Since 2008 he has published work in [ΦPMK], *Entefktirio, Lifo, Athens Voice, Unfollow* and others. 'The Chaos' is part of the upcoming poetry project titled *Is* ([ΦPMK]).

Iordanis Papadopoulos is author of two books of poetry, *Bras de Fer* (Gutenberg, 2015) and *The mountain and the poet have got no clue* (Roes, 2009). Recent poems can be found online and in literary magazines. He is a member of live art group KangarooCourt.

Stephanos Papadopoulos is author of three books of poems. *Lost Days, Hôtel-Dieu,* and *The Black Sea,* as well as editor and co-translator (with Katerina Anghelaki-Rooke) of Derek Walcott's *Selected Poems* into Greek. He was awarded a Civitella Ranieri Fellowship for *The Black Sea* and in 2014 he received the Jeannette Haien Ballard Writer's Prize, selected by Mark Strand.

Eleni Philippou is a poet published in a number of journals and anthologies.

Stamatis Polenakis is author of *The Hand of Time* (Omvros, 2002), *The Blue Horses of Franz Marc* (Odos Panos, 2006), *Notre Dame* (Odos Panos, 2008), *The Odessa Steps* (Mikri Arktos, 2012), *The glorious stone* (Mikri Arktos, 2014). His poems have been published in Greek literary reviews as well as in the UK, US and Switzerland.

Nick Potamitis was born in 1975 and grew up in north London.

George Prevedourakis has published two poetry collections: *Timegraph* (Planodion, 2011) and *Kleftiko* (Panoptiko, 2013). Poems, texts and translations have been published in various literary magazines.

Theodoros Rakopoulos has published two collections of poetry, a hybrid book that explores the conspiracy theory in texts between prose and poetry and collection of short stories. He has been awarded the State Prize and the National Centre for Books prize for debut author.

Kiriakos Sifiltzoglou has published three poetry collections: *To Each His Own Grave* (Gavrielides, 2007), *Half Truths* (Melani, 2012), *In the Style of An Indian* (Melani, 2014).

Eleni Sikélianòs is author of seven poetry books, most recently *The Loving Detail of the Living & the Dead* (Coffee House, 2013), and two hybrid memoirs (*The Book of Jon,* City Lights, and *You Animal Machine,* Coffee House). She has received two National Endowment for the Arts Awards, a Fulbright Fellowship, and the National Poetry Series. Her work has been translated into over a dozen languages. 'Survey: Phototrope' is from *The Loving Detail of the Living & the Dead* and is reprinted with the kind permission of The Permissions Company, Inc., on behalf of Coffee House Press.

A. E. Stallings is an American poet who has lived in Greece since 1999. She is a MacArthur fellow. Her most recent collection is *Olives*.

Yiannis Stiggas has published five poetry collections: *The vagrancy of blood*, (Gavrielidis, 2004), *Vision will start again* (Kedros, 2006), *An even wound* (Kedros, 2009), *The Road to the newspaper kiosk* (Mikri Arktos, 2012) and *I saw Rubik's cube eaten up* (Mikri Arktos, 2014). He has read at various international poetry festivals. His poems have been translated in German, French, Swedish, Spanish, English, Serbian and Bulgarian.

Barnaby Tideman: 'These extracts are taken from Geraneia, an 'epic poem' I'm writing inspired by fragments, remains, and reformations: ['memories of the future' up against the 'past lives' of the psyche, set in landscapes coloured by catastrophic change.] Geraneia is the name of a Greek mountain I lived under in the city-state of Megara, and means 'mountain of the cranes' [(being, supposedly, the place where cranes landed after Deucalion's flood)]; the poem moves through Greece, Italy, and Britain, following various strands of time.

Maria Topali has published three poetry collections, the hybrid essay *A Quatre Mains* in collaboration with Konstantine Matsoukas (Gavrielides, 2013), the musical *The Dance of the Middle Class* and the pamphlet *My words, Oratorio for Chorus and Voices in the Centre of Athens* (Nefeli, 2015). She has translated Rilke, Enzensberger, Frisch amongst others and has taught poetry translation at the European Centre of Translation and Literature in Athens.

Tryfon Tolides' first book, *An Almost Pure Empty Walking*, was a 2005 National Poetry Series selection, published by Penguin in 2006. In 2009, he received a Lannan Foundation Writer Residency in Marfa, Texas.

Thanasis Triaridis has published more than forty books of narratives, plays and essays — amongst which *honeyed lemons — the will and testament of the horny people* and *the verdant diamonds * the sunset of the horny people*. His plays have been staged in theatres in Athens and Thessaloniki. He has published approximately three hundred essays, articles and other texts. His work has been translated into English, French, German and Italian.

Thomas Tsalapatis' debut poetry collection *Dawn is a Massacre, Mister Krak* (Ekati, 2011) was awarded the State Literary Award for Best Newcomer in 2012. His second collection *Alba* was published in 2015. His poems and other texts have been translated into English, Italian, French and Spanish.

George Ttoouli is a London-born poet, academic and editor of Cretan and Cypriot descent, living in Coventry. With Simon Turner he co-edits Gist and Piths, a sporadic blogzine. His most recent project is *The Apple Anthology*, co-edited with Yvonne Reddick (Nine Arches Press, 2013).

Universal Jenny was born 2 October 2013. Attempting a transcendence of individual and collective consciousness in terms of either/or, her poetry seeks to narrate the impact of historical momentum on actually existing life. Universal Jenny is committed to the insights of symbolic characters, such as Brecht's Pirate Jenny, and of real people whose passage through political humanity has expanded the remit of the possible.

Steve Willey is a London-based poet and Lecturer in Creative and Critical Writing at Birkbeck, University of London. He is the author of *Elegy* (Veer Books, 2013) and *Sea Fever* (Knives Forks and Spoons, forthcoming 2015). His ongoing project *Living In* has been published as 'In Sufficiency' in *Extraordinary Rendition* (Or Books, 2015), 'Mirror: Flag' in US web magazine *Spiral Orb* (2014), as 'Signals: Letters to Palestine' in *Dear World and Everyone In It* (Bloodaxe Books, 2013), and as 'Slogans' in *Better Than Language* (Ganzfeld Press, 2011).